Management Extra

RECRUITMENT AND SELECTION

Management Extra

RECRUITMENT AND SELECTION

AMSTERDAM • BOSTON • HEIDELBERG • LONDON • NEW YORK • OXFORD • PARIS • SAN DIEGO • SAN FRANCISCO • SINGAPORE • SYDNEY • TOKYO

Elsevier Butterworth-Heinemann
Linacre House, Jordan Hill, Oxford OX2 8DP
30 Corporate Drive, Burlington, MA 01803

First published 2005

British Library Cataloguing in Publication Data
A catalogue record for this book is available from the British Library

Library of Congress Cataloguing in Publication Data
A catalogue record for this book is available from the Library of Congress

ISBN 0 7506 6689 7

For information on all Elsevier Butterworth-Heinemann publications
visit our website at www.books.elsevier.com

Printed and bound in Italy

Working together to grow
libraries in developing countries

www.elsevier.com | www.bookaid.org | www.sabre.org

ELSEVIER   BOOK AID
            International   Sabre Foundation

Contents

Activities

Figures

Tables

Series preface

*'I hear I forget
I see I remember
I do I understand'*

Galileo

Management Extra is designed to help you put ideas into practice. Each book in the series is full of thought-provoking ideas, examples and theories to help you understand the key management concepts of our time. There are also activities to help you see how the concepts work in practice.

The text and activities are organised into bite-sized themes or topics. You may want to review a theme at a time, concentrate on gaining understanding through the text or focus on the activities whilst dipping into the text for reference.

The activities are varied. Some are work-based, asking you to consider changing, developing and extending your current practice. Others ask you to reflect on new ideas, check your understanding or assess the application of concepts in different contexts. The activities will give you a valuable opportunity to practise various techniques in a safe environment.

And, finally, exploring and sharing your ideas with others can be very valuable in making the most of this resource.

More information on using this book as part of a course or programme of learning is available on the Management Extra website.

www.managementextra.co.uk

Recruiting the right people

The red-hot competition for talented employees is no longer news. Employers everywhere recognise that they must evolve better recruitment, selection and retention strategies if they are to compete effectively with their rivals for the best people.

They are also aware that recruitment and selection is a skilled and costly process which even in the smallest organisation needs to be structured and organised to:

◆ attract people with ability and potential from a wide pool of talent

◆ enable the selector to predict how a candidate will perform on the job as accurately as possible.

Responsibility for recruitment and selection, once the preserve of the HR team, is now usually devolved to, or shared jointly with, the line manager. This makes sense – the line manager has detailed knowledge of the job, the skills that the post-holder will need and the culture of the team the new recruit will join. But the shift in responsibility has implications for the skills and knowledge of the line manager.

This is a book for line managers. It discusses current practices in recruitment and selection and offers advice on how to take an approach that is strategically focused, effective, fair and based on best practice.

Your objectives are to:

◆ Determine the essential stages of the recruitment and selection process and the manager's role within it

◆ Consider how to take account of equality and diversity issues, including legislation and related codes of practice

◆ Assess alternative approaches to external recruitment for addressing shortfalls in the pool of skills, knowledge, and experience

◆ Profile a job role and develop information that describes the vacancy in fair, clear and accurate terms

◆ Evaluate methods for attracting people from a wide pool of talent

◆ Explore methods for selecting the candidate who is likely to perform most effectively

◆ Develop a process for ensuring a positive start for a new employee.

1 Essentials of recruitment and selection

Let's start by making a distinction between selection practices and recruitment strategies.

Recruitment is best described as the way in which an organisation tries to source or attract the people from whom it will ultimately make selections. Recruitment strategies include efforts to reach better pools of candidates and to sell the organisation as an employer of choice.

Selection is about choosing between job candidates. It is about how to make a fair and accurate assessment of the strengths and weaknesses of applicants and how to identify the candidate who is most likely to perform well in the job.

It's also important to note that external recruitment is only one option for solving resource shortfalls in your organisation. Most organisations now deploy a variety of flexible working practices and HR planning techniques to help match the supply of people to peaks and trough in demand.

> **The purpose of selection is to match people to work. It is the most important element in any organisation's management of people simply because it is not possible to optimise the effectiveness of human resources, by whatever method, if there is a less than adequate match.**
>
> **Roberts (1997)**

In this first theme, you will:

- **Identify the main stages in the recruitment and selection process and consider the central role of the line manager**
- Analyse the strengths and weaknesses of the recruitment and selection process in your organisation
- Assess how the legal framework for recruitment and selection supports the promotion of equal opportunities and a diverse workforce
- Explore alternatives to external recruitment for addressing shortfalls in an organisation's pool of skills, knowledge and experience

The recruitment and selection process

Getting it wrong is not an option – if the wrong person is appointed it can affect teamwork, while morale and motivation take a nosedive. Your productivity goes down and there are sharp questions that must be answered – probably by you.

From the business point of view, the cost of getting it wrong can be counted in money, as recruitment is so expensive. At the end of the day it can destroy profitability.

Recruitment – an expensive business

It should be noted that the costs of time and lost productivity are no less important or real than the costs associated with paying cash to vendors for services such as advertising or temporary staff. These are very real costs to the employer.

These calculations will easily reach 150% of the employee's annual compensation figure. The cost will be significantly higher (200% to 250% of annual compensation) for managerial and sales positions.

To put this in perspective, let's assume the average salary of employees in a given company is $50,000 per year. Taking the cost of turnover at 150% of salary, the cost of turnover is then $75,000 per employee who leaves the company. For the mid-sized company of 1,000 employees that has a 10% annual rate of turnover, the annual cost of turnover is $7.5 million!

Do you know any CEO who would not want to add $7.5 million to their revenue? And by the way, most of the figure would be carried over to the profit line as well. What about a company with 10,000 employees? The cost of turnover equals $75 million!

Source: *Bliss* (2000)

Some of the main factors you and your organisation need to consider when calculating the cost of recruitment are given in Table 1.1. As you can see, they go far beyond the direct costs of hiring a new person. Clearly, with the costs involved, recruitment can never be undertaken in a haphazard way. A systematic approach is essential.

Departing employee	Recruitment and selection	New employee
Temporary cover for vacant post and lower productivity	Manager's time spent in analysing the vacancy and specifying the job	Induction and job skills training
Administration costs for departing employee – payroll, pensions, etc.	Time spent in briefing/working with external agencies	Manager/employee's time spent in orientating new person
Lost skills and investment in training	Direct costs of working with external agencies	Administration costs of new employee – payroll, pensions, etc.
Loss of goodwill from customers	Direct advertising costs	Cost of the new employee being less than 100 per cent productive for weeks/months
Possible downturn in morale of remaining employees	Administration costs – sending out job information, letters, arranging selection events, etc.	Disruption to the department as the new person gets up to speed
	Manager's time – shortlisting, interviewing, selection, taking up references	Cost of any new equipment such as company car, mobile phone, laptop, etc.
	Training costs – ensuring everyone has the necessary skills to recruit	

Table 1.1 *Costs to consider when calculating the cost of recruitment*

A structure for recruiting and selecting employees

Figure 1.1 provides a structure for the recruitment and selection process. It's a fairly standard approach and you may use something similar already. Every step is important in giving you the best opportunity of attracting the best – people with ability and potential. While you may not be able to change your recruitment process, you have full control over what you contribute to it.

1 **Determine whether recruitment is necessary.** It may be that the vacancy can be filled in some other way. Valuable information can be obtained by conducting an exit interview with the person who is leaving. You can then look at how the post could be filled from within, for example, through redeployment or flexible working.

2 **Analyse the job.** Adopting a methodology for job analysis establishes what is required of the post-holder. This provides the information you will need in order to specify the job and the person best suited to fill the vacancy.

3 **Write a job description or competency profile, and person specification.** The job description states the purpose, responsibilities and conditions of the job. The person specification provides a framework of the qualities and abilities that best fit the job. As an alternative to the job description, some organisations are using competency profiles. These state the competencies for the role, rather than listing specific tasks and duties.

4 **Decide on the most appropriate application and selection methods.** The common choice is between the application form and the curriculum vitae (CV). You also need to decide at this stage how to select the candidate – through interview alone, or using some form of selection test.

5 **Decide how to attract candidates.** Making decisions about how to market a vacancy is crucial – it ensures you reach your potential recruits, and mistakes can be costly.

6 **Market the job.** Once the decision on where to market has been taken, it is also important that you decide how to market. This means ensuring that any advertisement is fair and representative of both the job and your organisation.

7 **Sift and shortlist applications.** This means reducing the number of applicants to a manageable number for selection. If too few people are carried forward to the next stage it restricts your choice; too many and it wastes time and leads to confusion.

8 **Hold selection interviews and/or events.** The selection method should have been agreed earlier. The event itself must be well managed, not only to analyse the match between candidate and job, but also to give a good impression of the organisation they may be joining.

9 **Make a decision and offer.** The decision about who to appoint must be based on facts and evidence, not gut reaction or instinct. Once the decision has been taken, the successful candidate can be informed face to face or by phone, and always in writing.

10 **Take up references.** References are usually requested once a conditional offer has been made and they are a vital part of the selection process. References can be obtained by phone or letter but, as a manager, you need to be aware of the potential pitfalls.

11 **Induct and train the new employee.** A good start is essential if you want the person to be effective in their new role quickly. Thorough induction helps to build loyalty and commitment, thus increasing the chances of retaining their skills within the organisation.

12 **Involve the same people throughout the recruitment process.** This will help you achieve consistency and consensus.

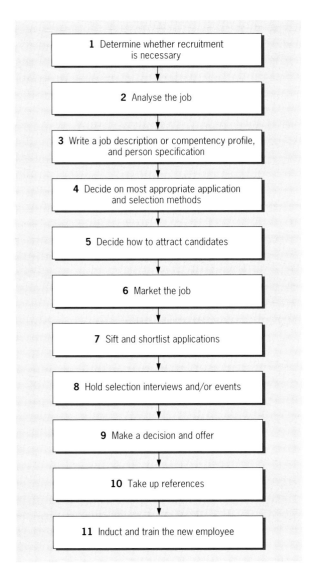

Figure 1.1 *The recruitment and selection process*

The manager's role

Your role in recruitment will largely depend on how sophisticated the human resource (HR) structures are within the organisation. A dedicated HR department will probably take a lead role in recruiting staff and may have tried and tested procedures, roles and responsibilities. However, you still have important responsibilities as a manager.

Whether you have an HR function or not, as the manager of the recruit, you should be involved from the very start. You have the clearest idea of what the team is trying to achieve and the skills and qualities needed to enhance that effort.

You are also the person who will be responsible for the new employee, so you are in the best position to judge:

◆ which candidate has the most suitable starting skills

◆ which candidate has the potential to develop in the role

◆ which candidate could best enhance the team's working practices

◆ which candidate will benefit the team/department/organisation in the long term.

In today's employment environment managers must take extra care to avoid costly employment mistakes.

Mistakes managers can make are:

◆ looking at the role in isolation, without considering any organisational needs for flexibility and change

◆ leaving the process to chance – your gut instinct will tell you who's the best person to appoint at the time

◆ believing everything a candidate writes on their application and believing everything a candidate tells you at interview

◆ making sure the person you choose has a similar background, education and interests as you do, particularly golf, football and fine wines

◆ assuming that high academic achievement equals high work performance

◆ appointing the most highly qualified person for the job, rather than the most suitably qualified one

◆ believing that candidates must impress you – that the image you portray is immaterial

◆ ignoring the need to take up references – it'll just delay the process

◆ throwing them in at the deep end on day one to let them find their feet – it's a good test of character.

Activity 1
Employment figures

Objective

This activity will help you to establish the need for effective recruitment procedures in times of high employment.

Task

1   Read the following extract taken from an article that appeared in *The Sunday Times.*

Recruitment and high employment

When (unemployment) edged below 1m last week, it was a cause for celebration, occasioning a press conference featuring Tony Blair and half his cabinet. What caught my eye was the fact that, for the first time in nearly 30 years, there are more job vacancies in the economy than there are unemployed people to fill them. There are 390,000 officially recorded Job-centre positions. These, according to government statisticians, account for only one third of all vacant jobs in the economy.

Multiplying the number of vacancies by three gives us a grand total of 1.17m vacancies, which is nearly 200,000 more than the claimant count.

What are the vacancy figures telling us? Part of the message is indeed that the labour market is getting tighter. There are 85,000 Job-centre vacancies in London and south-east England which, applying the rule of three, implies about a quarter of a million jobs are going spare.

But there are also, and this is where it gets puzzling, 23,000 Job-centre vacancies (69,000 in total) in north east England, where the unemployment rate is nearly four times that of the south-east. Vacancies relative to the size of the workforce are actually higher in the north-east than the south-east.

It would be wrong to think this is a case of a lot of unattractive jobs never being filled. Part of the reason is that, for low-paid jobs, travel costs are a serious disincentive. Another is that Britons are immobile when it comes to travelling even short distances for work reasons.

There are other reasons. When I leaf through *The Sunday Times* appointment section out of curiosity, not only could I not begin to do most of the jobs advertised, but I cannot even understand the job descriptions. There are certain types of jobs for which the supply of suitable people will always lag a long way behind demand.

Source: *Smith* (2001)

2 Use the information you have just read, as well as your own understanding of the issues, to list at least six reasons why it is so important that you have effective recruitment procedures.

Effective recruitment procedures are important because:

Feedback

There are many reasons to support the need for effective recruitment procedures. The following are among the most important:

- ◆ To widen the pool of talent on which you can draw in times of high employment

- ◆ To stand a better chance of selecting someone who is keen and enthusiastic, because you have more people from whom to select

- ◆ To make your firm attractive in geographical areas of skill shortage

- ◆ To provide you with a competitive edge over businesses offering similar terms and conditions when skills are short in certain occupational areas

- ◆ To attract good people, because a well-planned process makes it clear what is expected of the job-holder

- ◆ To recruit someone who will stay with you because transparent standards of performance for the role make it easier to make a close match between the person and the job

- ◆ To encourage people to travel further, even relocate, to work for you

- ◆ To reduce costs since the most suitable person is more likely to be recruited first time around – and stay with you.

Activity 2
A recruitment analysis tool

Objectives

This activity will help you to:

◆ look closely at the people involved in recruitment in your organisation

◆ consider whether you should take a more active role.

Task

The following checklist is constructed from the recruitment and selection process in Figure 1.1. Identify who is involved at each stage when you recruit for your own department. Tick the relevant columns.

Stage	Senior manager	HR/ Personnel	You i.e. the line manager	Other managers	Others: agencies, employees
Deciding whether recruitment is necessary	☐	☐	☐	☐	☐
Conducting a job analysis	☐	☐	☐	☐	☐
Writing a job description or profile, and person specification	☐	☐	☐	☐	☐
Deciding on the most appropriate application and selection methods	☐	☐	☐	☐	☐
Deciding how to attract candidates	☐	☐	☐	☐	☐
Marketing the job	☐	☐	☐	☐	☐
Sifting and shortlisting applications	☐	☐	☐	☐	☐
Holding/taking part in selection interview and/or events	☐	☐	☐	☐	☐
Making the decision and job offer	☐	☐	☐	☐	☐
Taking up references	☐	☐	☐	☐	☐
Inducting and training the new employee	☐	☐	☐	☐	☐

Feedback

The boxes you have ticked will depend on the size and structure of your organisation. For example, if you have a human resources department, they may drive the recruitment process. Even if that is the case, it is important that you are involved in the process as much as possible. You are the one who is going to have to manage the new recruit, therefore you must feel happy with the way the decision is reached. In fact HR should be there to support and underpin what you do – not the other way round.

If you have ticks dotted all over the table, then you should be concerned. This implies there is no consistency: no one person or department is in overall control. This might mean, for example, that the job description does not reflect the job analysis and any recruitment advertising might not be in line with the person specification. Consistency is the key to success.

As the manager your next steps are to look at the stages you are not involved in, and consider ways you can take a more active role. You should also consider the possible consequences of not being involved. You may end up with an unsatisfactory new employee who cannot do the job, does not fit in with the team and takes up your valuable time as you try to manage this below-par performer.

Note below any action you feel you need to take to make your role more active. Who do you need to talk to?

Action	*By when*

The legal framework

While a sound recruitment process helps in appointing the most capable person, it is also essential to ensure that you fulfil all your legal requirements. The law that governs recruitment is not designed to constrict an organisation's choice, it is rather to assure fair access to jobs.

Recruitment and selection is not just covered by national law, it is increasingly subject to European Union legislation as well. It is important that you, as a manager, keep up to date with any changes. For example, laws covering discrimination on grounds of race, gender and disability have been with us for years.

Did you know that new EU legislation is giving rights to other minority groups where discrimination has gone unpunished in the past?

◆ Europe has introduced the Transsexual Directive, which prohibits discrimination against transsexuals at any stage of the process of gender reassignment in all member countries.

◆ The European Convention on Human Rights has been incorporated into national law. To find out more about the European Convention on Human Rights, see www.humanrights.coe.int.

◆ The EC Framework Directive is affecting national law in terms of prohibiting discrimination in the areas of religion or belief, sexual orientation and age.

What can go wrong?

The most common problem that can occur during recruitment is that an applicant experiences discrimination. This may be deliberate or unintended.

There are two main forms of discrimination:

◆ Direct discrimination arises when a person treats another person or group of people less favourably in a particular situation because of their race, religion, ethnic origin, gender, marital status, disability, responsibility for dependants, sexual orientation or gender reassignment.

◆ Indirect discrimination means specifying a requirement or condition which, although applied equally to persons of all groups, is such that:

– a considerably smaller proportion of one particular group of people can comply with it than the proportion of people outside that group

– it is to the detriment of the person or group who cannot comply with it and

– it cannot be shown to be justifiable on the basis of merit/ability or other objective criteria.

Why good practice matters

The law sets the parameters for good practice and protects people and organisations from unfairness and inequality. Adopting good

> **Businesses are no longer thinking of diversity as about equality in terms of the law and compliance, they are seeing it as an issue of merit.**
>
> **Amin (2003)**

equal opportunities practice within your recruitment and selection process matters from a commercial point of view.

♦ You have more people with talent to select from. An organisation with a wide employee base presents an attractive image to a greater diversity of potential recruits.

♦ Creativity is enhanced as more diverse ideas are brought to day-to-day decision making and problem solving within your team, rather than having a narrow outlook in terms of age, gender and ethnicity.

♦ Morale and motivation increase as employees see you recruiting people on factors that matter. In other words, what they know, not who they know. This in turn reduces employee turnover and the need for yet more costly recruitment.

♦ Your customer service standards improve and your customer base can grow. A greater empathy develops between staff and customers, so your reputation is enhanced.

♦ There is less chance of being prosecuted under equal opportunities laws, which means that fines and costs, as well as bad publicity, are avoided.

Table 1.2 highlights the importance of so-called minority groups in the workplace.

The percentage of working women with children under 10	49%
The number of people with disabilities in the UK	6 million
The ethnic group with the highest percentage achieving one A level or more	Chinese
In 10 years' time, the percentage of the working population over 45	40%
The number of people who have experienced age discrimination	8 million

Table 1.2 *The situation in the UK – did you know?*

Race discrimination

Commission for Racial Equality (CRE) News Release – 12 January 2001

Post Office condemned for discriminatory recruitment practices
The Post Office paid £19,757.19 in damages today after management at their Preston office were found to have selectively applied performance tests, leading to racial discrimination...

The Tribunal found that Mrs Nagamani Mallidi, a postal worker of Indian origin, had received 'less favourable treatment' than her white counterparts. She was asked to take a written aptitude test in order to remain in employment, when a number of comparable white employees were given temporary or permanent contracts without having to take the test. The Tribunal stated that they were extremely unhappy about the way the Post Office operated in terms of its treatment of Asian employees. They said that the Post Office had failed to explain why the test was applied so rigorously in certain cases and not in others.

When Mrs Mallidi made a complaint of racial discrimination, the management failed to investigate the matter with any seriousness. The Tribunal found this failure to address legitimate complaints to be direct discrimination on the grounds of race.

Source: *CRE* (2001)

Sex discrimination

**Equal Opportunities Commission (EOC) News Release –
2 August 2000**

**Award of £7,000 compensation for sex discrimination
confirmed**

A panel wirer who was prevented from applying for a job because she was a woman was awarded £7,000 compensation, the Equal Opportunities Commission announced today.

An Employment Appeal Tribunal dismissed an appeal, lodged by Roselec Ltd, against the Tribunal's decision. However, Ms Cashmore has yet to receive any compensation from Roselec as the company has gone into voluntary insolvency.

Ms Cashmore won her sex discrimination claim in January 1999 against Roselec Ltd – an engineering company, and Anystaff Recruitment Ltd – an employment agency. She had approached the agency about a vacancy for a panel wirer with Roselec. But the agency was subsequently told by Roselec that there was no such vacancy and that the work was of a heavy nature, for which a man would be more suitable. When Ms Cashmore asked an employee of Anystaff Recruitment to provide a statement in support of her application to the tribunal he refused to do so. Anystaff have paid her the compensation they owed.

Julie Mellor, Chair of the Equal Opportunities Commission, said:

'The discrimination Ms Cashmore experienced was clearly based on outdated preconceptions about what kinds of work women are capable of doing. This is an example of how sex stereotyping leads to wasted talent and unfulfilled potential. The EOC believes that each individual's ability to do any particular job should be the only basis on which they are judged. Opening up different roles and opportunities to women and men will not only benefit individuals but also the economy – closing skills gaps and providing employers with a larger pool of potential employees.'

Source: *EOC* (2000)

Equal opportunities for all

The following will help you make certain that your recruitment policy conforms to good equal opportunities practice:

◆ Make sure your organisation's equal opportunities policy complies with current legislation and best practice.

◆ Be involved personally at every step of the recruitment and selection process – and don't let others dip in and out, as consistency is the key.

◆ Make sure everyone clearly understands what's involved and is trained in key skills, especially interviewing techniques.

◆ Look into ways of widening access to jobs, for example by working with local community groups and carrying out projects with local schools.

◆ Assess ways of making your organisation more attractive, for example by offering flexible working and reviewing local childcare options. Think about introducing a system of 'work tasters' so people have an idea of what it's like to work for you.

◆ Consider changing the way you recruit for posts. For example, if this is the traditional route of CV and interview, look at the feasibility of using application forms and testing.

◆ Discuss with others the idea of introducing 'positive action'. This is the practice of encouraging members of certain ethnic, gender or other specific groups to apply for positions previously held exclusively or mainly by members of different groups over the previous 12 months. Lead by example and only discriminate on the grounds of merit, capability and performance.

Policy essentials
Make sure your own equal opportunities policy covers these areas:

◆ purpose/statement of intent/commitment

◆ objectives – what you are trying to achieve

◆ definitions such as discrimination or victimisation

◆ its importance – how it will benefit the organisation, its people and the community

◆ who is responsible for the policy at a senior level

◆ what is covered, for example, vacancy advertising, recruitment and selection, promotion and training

◆ positive action

◆ record keeping.

Discriminate only on relevant factors such as ability and potential, never on irrelevancies like gender, race or age.

Activity 3
Equal opportunities in recruitment

Objective

Use this activity to assess the importance of applying good equal opportunities practice when recruiting.

Background

Read the following extract from a report produced by the Chartered Institute of Personnel and Development (CIPD).

> **Ageism in the workplace**
> Ageism is still evident in the recruitment area, despite the publication of the Government's Code of Practice on Age Diversity in Employment in the early summer of 1999, which aimed to reduce the incidents of age discrimination in the workplace by targeting employers. One in eight workers report that they have been discouraged from applying for a job in the last year because the recruitment advertisement contained either an upper age range, or implied that the applicant needed to be a certain age by using wording such as 'young'.

Source: *Compton-Edwards* (2001)

This extract suggests that discrimination against older workers is common, particularly in recruitment advertising.

Task

1 In what ways do you think discrimination against older workers can arise during recruitment?

2 Why is discrimination against older workers bad management practice?

Age discrimination arises because:	Ageism in recruitment is bad because:

Feedback

You may have noted down some of the following ideas:

1   Discrimination can arise in a number of ways. If age is not requested on application forms, it can be implied through insisting on a certain level of experience. Application forms sometimes request an applicant's date of birth. Even if this is not the case, some people involved in shortlisting are put off by people who qualified years ago. Many managers still like to recruit in their own image and prefer someone of a similar age. Also, because the first impression is so important, they may be affected by physical appearance. An older worker may not represent their mental image of the ideal candidate. In some cases, managers are actually frightened of an older worker, believing their wealth of experience could put their own role in jeopardy. Conversely, they regard older workers as best suited to low pay, low status jobs.

2   It is likely to become illegal to discriminate against someone because of their age, as it is already with gender, race and disability.

    However, by practising discrimination against older workers, the manager is potentially missing out on a raft of skills and experience not available in other staff. Older workers can bring an experienced perspective to day-to-day decision making and a better skills balance to the department/ organisation as a whole. By employing a good age range of staff you are more likely to reflect your own customer base and may attract older customers, many of whom have enormous spending power. Older staff can reduce turnover costs because they are less likely to be pursuing a career and this continuity can help the continuity of the business. This is particularly important at times when younger staff are scarce and may be lured away by employment opportunities elsewhere.

Activity 4
Conducting a SWOT analysis

Objective

Use this activity to assess recruitment and selection practices in your own department, using a SWOT analysis.

Background

A SWOT analysis is a way of understanding the organisation's current position in terms of:

◆ Strengths – the capabilities that provide a definite advantage over the competition

◆ Weaknesses – the things the business does less well

◆ Opportunities – favourable environmental factors that open up new possibilities

◆ Threats – unfavourable environmental factors that may undermine success.

As with any other business process, a SWOT analysis can be conducted on recruitment and selection.

During your analysis, bear in mind the following:

◆ Strengths and weaknesses are usually associated with internal factors, in the department/organisation, over which you can have some level of control. They may include the employment policies, processes, involvement of others.

◆ Opportunities and threats are associated with external factors, over which you have less control. They may include the structure of the labour market, and economic and demographic conditions in the community from which you draw employees.

Task

Conduct a SWOT analysis on recruitment and selection within your own department. You may need to talk to colleagues, perhaps in the human resources department, to find out the situation for your organisation.

Strengths	Weaknesses

Opportunities	Threats

Feedback

Here are the results of a SWOT analysis conducted on recruitment in the IT department of a small manufacturing company. See how your organisation compares.

Strengths	Weaknesses
Good recruitment policy	Too few line managers involved in recruitment
Strong HR department	Managers lack training in, and experience of, recruiting
Well-defined job descriptions	
Management competency framework in place	Limited methods of attracting candidates
Good working environment – good selling point	Over-reliance on one recruitment consultancy
Good diversity of employees – age, ethnicity, etc.	Induction not detailed enough – problem with retention?
Equal opportunities policy in place	
Career development opportunities – selling point	

Opportunities	Threats
More freedom of movement across EU – attract staff from abroad	Better pay abroad – especially France and Germany
Growth of industry and housing in local area – source of recruits	Lack of skilled people coming out of colleges – in demand everywhere
Desire for people to work flexibly – we can offer it	Increase in head hunting from competitors
Ability/willingness to attract staff of all backgrounds (our track record)	Ability of others to offer working with the latest technology – we're not in that market
Compliance with EU Directives ahead of time – a caring employer – we need to market this	NB – competition from Third World may undermine whole business – no need for recruitment!

Alternatives to external recruitment

You have to consider very carefully whether you need to recruit externally when an employee leaves. In this section you consider the options for solving your shortage in skills, knowledge or resources from within your organisation.

Conducting an exit interview

As the name suggests, exit interviews are carried out with a departing employee. These can be of enormous value to both you and the organisation. It is an opportunity to deal with the administrative details for the leaver, and to wish them well. However, it also gives you the chance to find out the real reasons why they are leaving. You can identify any problems the jobholder encountered and determine the real requirements of the job being vacated. In other words, rather than just relying on a job description, which can be out of date, it is a chance to find out what the role actually entails. This information is then useful when you consider whether the role should be restructured or whether the leaver needs to be replaced at all.

An exit interview could follow this line of questioning:

- ◆ 'Did the day-to-day work activities match the job description?'
- ◆ 'Did internal or external pressures force you to concentrate on unimportant or low priority tasks?'
- ◆ 'Did you have too much to do and not enough time, or was there too little work, which meant you were bored?'
- ◆ 'Is there a better way of organising the work tasks?'
- ◆ 'Could elements of the job be carried out differently, such as using technology?'
- ◆ 'Did you have any difficulties with people on the team?'

Once you have the answers to these questions, you can look at the situation afresh.

Considering your options

It may be obvious from the exit interview and discussions with others that the job requires a new full-time employee. You may feel, however, that you can take a different approach to solve your problem. The options available will largely be influenced by existing policies and practices in your organisation.

19

Promotion from within

Promoting an existing employee is a useful option to consider. In a work environment where reducing management positions may restrict people's opportunity to progress, it can give a positive message to the workforce. If the promotion is handled well, it can increase staff morale. This means the person is fully trained and remunerated for the additional responsibility.

It can also encourage an employee to stay as it puts across the positive message that career paths do exist within the organisation. You must base the decision about whom to promote on objective criteria and be seen to be fair. An effective appraisal system can aid in this decision making, as can a process of succession planning.

The potential pitfalls of internal recruitment

Bear in mind these points when considering internal recruitment:

Internal recruitment may lead to existing inequalities in employment opportunities being reinforced, such as lack of women in senior positions. There is a danger that people are promoted too quickly or beyond their capability. There is the added concern that if an employee is an effective worker in one area, their manager may be reluctant to let them go. This situation can lead to demotivation as people see that their hard work is not rewarded.

A potentially critical problem in times of change is that long-term career development may not be appropriate when new and urgently needed skills are not available within the existing workforce. For example, major financial institutions in the City of London had to change recruitment policies rapidly and recruit externally in order to attract the skills required after deregulation of the industry.

Source: *adapted from Beardwell and Holden* (1997)

Redeployment

Another option you have is to redeploy someone with the required skills from another part of the organisation. This can be on a permanent basis or a temporary basis through secondment. While this may seem the most cost-effective solution, it is unlikely that one person would have all the necessary skills so some form of training will have to form part of the solution. In addition, if it is poorly handled, redeployment can be regarded as exploiting the workforce – making already stretched resources stretch even further.

Overtime working

This may be a solution for the short term. You might use overtime in an area where there are skills shortages and you are having problems filling the post with the right calibre replacement. Overtime can be popular with staff if it is voluntary and paid, but people cannot be pressurised to take on additional responsibility, especially without any reward.

If the job is highly skilled, it is likely that the people working overtime will require training. With these additional costs and the administration involved in organising the work, it can be an expensive option that does not actually solve the underlying problem.

Flexible working

This involves looking at a new framework for the way working time is structured. For example, if an exit interview highlights that the work was less intensive than you thought, part-time or reduced-hours working may be an option. If you have two part-time employees who each have the relevant skills, you could offer the post as a job-share. Indeed this may be an attractive option for full-timers who you know would like to reduce their hours.

The growth in flexible working

Flexible working has many benefits in today's workplace when increasingly people are looking for a better balance between their home and work life. More women than ever are working yet still have the major responsibility for childcare. At the other end of the spectrum, the issue of caring for the elderly is a growing concern.

An increasing number of people wish to take time away from the workplace to study or follow other interests, rather than commit to an organisation five days a week.

> **Over 38% of mothers and more than one in ten fathers have given up or turned down a job because of their caring responsibilities.**
> **EOC (2004)**

Research shows that having the ability to work flexibly is a real issue among young employees, as Table 1.3 highlights. This implies that young people will look for employment opportunities that offer some flexibility. This could mean that organisations not prepared to offer flexibility may lose out on talented recruits.

Adopting flexible work patterns indicates that an organisation is family friendly – it is good PR. On a practical level it adds to your ability to respond to change, sharpens your competitiveness, and may give you the edge in attracting and retaining valuable employees. Organisations are increasingly adopting flexible working as a way of recruiting and retaining valuable employees.

Area to consider	Yes	No
Do you think that parents should have a legal right to move from full-time to part-time working to look after young children?	90%	10%
Do you think that fathers should have time off work when the baby is first born?	93%	7%
Do you think that time off work will change the role of fathers within the family for the better?	84%	16%

Table 1.3 *Gallup survey on flexible working – results for the 16–34 age group*

Source: *EOC* (2001)

From your perspective as a manager, giving people the option to work flexibly can improve your results. People are more likely to enjoy coming to work and productivity improves as they aren't so tired and 'stale'. People who work flexibly are more likely to be committed, enthusiastic and willing to reward the organisation with hard work and effort.

In addition, refusing to allow employees to work flexibly is increasingly becoming an equal opportunities issue.

Flexible working and the law

EOC News Release – 7 November 2000

Inflexibility costs employer £18,000 and a valued employee
A consultancy firm that replaced a part-time personnel and payroll officer with a full-time worker and refused to consider her request to job-share is now paying her £18,000 compensation, the Equal Opportunities Commission announced today.

Karen Maloney, who comes from Leigh in Lancashire, had worked full-time for James R Knowles, a firm of construction contract consultants, for almost four years when she went on maternity leave. She returned to work, on a part-time basis, earlier than had been agreed, in order to help out at a difficult time. She then asked to continue working part-time, but soon after this had been agreed she was told she was going to be made redundant and replaced by a full-time worker.

When Ms Maloney objected and suggested a job-share instead, her manager said he did not believe in job-share arrangements. She was told she would be moved to another part-time position, but was not given details of the position, despite repeated requests.

The Liverpool Employment Tribunal decided that Ms Maloney had been discriminated against on the grounds of her sex and unfairly dismissed.

Source: *EOC* (2000b)

Some of the main flexible working methods are outlined below.

Common forms of flexible working

The advantages and disadvantages of these working methods are highlighted in Table 1.4.

Flexitime

Flexitime allows employees to choose their working hours around a central 'core' time when all employees must be at work. Core time depends on when the organisation is busiest and is often between the hours of 10am and 4pm. Employees can then choose the other hours they work from the full span of the working day, which can be from 8am to 8pm.

Starting and finishing times may vary, but hours should total a specified number within each month. With most schemes a small surplus of time can be carried over into the next month and be taken as a day's flexi-leave.

Job-sharing

Job-sharing allows two people to voluntarily share the duties and responsibilities of one full-time job. Unlike other forms of part-time work, job-sharing is not associated with low status or pay. There is an increasing acceptance of job-sharing in senior positions.

It tends to work best where duties and responsibilities can be clearly defined and undertaken with a reasonable degree of autonomy. Each of the sharers is employed on a permanent, part-time contract, with pay, holidays and other benefits divided according to the hours worked.

The job may be split in any one of several ways: the split day, the split week or working alternate weeks. In all cases there will need to be a hand over period, during which information is exchanged.

Term-time working

This is for employees with young children who are given the option of working during school term time only. Those eligible are usually defined as employees who are caring for children within a specified age range, for example, 5–14. It allows them to remain on a permanent full or part-time contract, while giving them the right to take unpaid leave during school holidays. They also maintain entitlement to service-related benefits and incremental pay. Pay itself is usually averaged out into 12 equal monthly instalments. Continuity of employment is not broken as long as the contracted hours are eight or more per week.

Annualised hours

The hours that the employee works are determined on the basis of the full working year. Employer and employee agree on the number of hours which will be needed during the year, and then decide on the best way to provide them.

An employee may be asked to work extra hours during regular peaks, but this would be balanced by a shorter working week during quiet periods. The hours worked during a week or month may vary, but salary remains constant from one month to the next.

Annual hours are generally split into fixed core times, which account for most of the hours, and unallocated hours where there is greater flexibility. The unallocated hours may then be planned at the beginning of every month.

> Productivity at the RAC increased by 8% after introducing annualised hours for its 1,250 service patrol and 500 call centre staff.

Source: *EOC* (2004)

Voluntarily reduced work time

This allows employees to reduce their hours of work voluntarily for a specified period, usually a reduction of between 5 per cent and 50 per cent. It can be arranged by shortening the working day or week, or by taking a block of time off during the year.

This can be useful for employees who suddenly find they are involved in a personal crisis, such as family illness. It is also useful for people studying for a qualification, which in the long term may benefit the organisation.

Home-based working

In this situation, the employee usually works some hours at home and others in the workplace. Using the broadly accepted definition of a teleworker, an individual who works at home for at least one day a week and in doing so uses a telephone and computer to do their job (DTI), the Spring 2001 Labour Force reported 2.2 million teleworkers in the UK or 7.4% of all employees (DTI 2002).

Bill Gates has claimed that by the year 2050, 50% of the working population will operate from home.

Handy (2001)

In most cases the employee is given the flexibility of managing their own workload as they wish, but often around core hours. This gives people the opportunity to work early mornings and evenings if they want to. This is a flexible option that can fit well with family life.

Form of work	Advantages	Disadvantages
Flexitime	Allows work to be geared to peaks and troughs of business	Can be abused if time is not recorded carefully
	Can improve staff morale as home/ work balance better managed	Can lead to disputes if some areas of the business use it and others don't
Job-sharing	A useful retention tool for employees with carer responsibilities	Needs a high level of communication and co-operation between sharers
	Can lead to greater creativity with the skills of two people	Only suitable where employees can be relatively autonomous
Term-time working	Attractive option to working parents	Can lead to complaints from others who do not have this flexibility
	Suitable for workload that shows seasonal variations	Can put other employees under pressure if work has to be covered
Annualised hours	Can reduce overtime working to cover busy periods	Long hours may be worked at busy periods leading to fatigue
	Staff can have additional leave at specified times of the year	Can take time to set up
Voluntarily reduced work time	Suitable for meeting a range of needs	Hours need to be negotiated with individuals – this can take time
	Best used where continuous cover is not a requirement	People can find it difficult to return full time at the end of the period
Home-based working	Reduces office space needed	Can be expensive to set up
	Good method for retaining highly skilled and motivated people	Needs a high level of trust between manager and employee

Table 1.4 *Advantages and disadvantages of flexible working*

Activity 5
Recruitment – only one option

Objective

Use this activity to assess the alternatives to filling a post with a permanent, full-time member of staff.

Case study

Read the following managerial deliberations.

> **Thinking out loud**
> Mike Smithfield handed in his notice last week because he got a better offer from a competitor company. In fact, I suspect the real reason is that he's just obtained a training qualification and wants to use it. Can't blame him for that. He leaves us in three weeks.

In fact, his job was going nowhere here. In the last five years most of our production has gone abroad, so the workforce has gone down from 600 to 150 employees. The maths show you the chance of applying training skills has been reduced. Also, the recent performance reviews have highlighted very little need for training, apart from on-the-job training. The needs that were highlighted are in very specialised areas, so we'd probably have to bring in an outside company to deliver on these anyway.

In fact, the company's still getting smaller. I know of five people who are being made redundant and won't be replaced as departments merge. We're being floated on the stock market next year, so we've got to be lean and fit. In fact, we're becoming just a base for sales and marketing.

Apart from the training, the rest of Mike's job is to do with payroll and recruitment. I was beginning to think that his job was shrinking. I could make it up to a full-time post by giving him Facilities to look after. That's not a full-time job either, although someone does do it on that basis at the moment.

But I've got a dilemma now. I've got half a job with Facilities, which is filled by a full-timer and two thirds of a job from Mike. Although payroll will shrink and there's not a lot of recruitment. What choices do I have?

Task

1   Why is it unlikely Mike needs to be replaced on a full-time permanent basis?

2   What other options are open to the manager?

Mike doesn't need to be replaced on a full-time, permanent basis because:

The manager's options are:

Feedback

You may agree with some of these ideas:

1 It's unlikely Mike needs to be replaced on a full-time basis as the job is shrinking and will probably continue to do so. There's very little, if any, training, which is what Mike wanted to do. As the company is getting leaner and fitter, it's unlikely recruitment will be a big part of the job. Also, as the workforce gets smaller so does the payroll. It seems the company is focused on flotation, so even in the medium-term, the job is unlikely to grow. However, what the manager must do is carry out an exit interview with Mike to hear what he has to say. The manager must also carry out a job analysis with Mike on the parts of the job that remain, to see exactly what's involved.

2 The manager has a number of options:

♦ There's the possibility of finding someone internally who is capable of carrying out the job on a part-time basis.

♦ There's the possibility of combining Mike's job with the Facilities job, and redeploying someone with some of the necessary skills who can be trained into this combined role. Or the manager could ask the person in charge of Facilities whether they would be prepared to take on the responsibility of Mike's job. This assumes Mike's remaining role will continue to shrink.

♦ Someone could be promoted into the combined role, so that even if the company is getting smaller, people see there are still career prospects available.

♦ There may be an option for offering the role to one of the five people who are about to be made redundant.

♦ The manager could change the way the job is worked and see if anyone would be interested in part-time working, job-sharing or even annualised hours. With the last option it would mean that any recruitment or training could be built in when needed.

Activity 6
The case for flexible working

Objective

Use this activity to consider the possibility of a current post within your department being worked on a flexible basis.

Task

1 Find out as much as you can about flexible working options. For example, flexi-time, job-sharing, term-time working, annualised hours and home-based working. Management and HR books will be useful. You can also search on the Internet.

2 What options does your organisation currently use? Which ones do you think your organisation may consider?

Options currently in use and under consideration:

3 Look at a current job or vacant post within your department. Decide which flexible working option is best suited to this post. Give reasons for your answer.

The best suited flexible working option and why:

Feedback

Whichever option you chose, you should have considered:

◆ its advantages and possible disadvantages

◆ the costs of implementation – in terms of money and people's time

◆ the impact on the department

◆ the benefits for the organisation, the department and the individual, for example, improved morale and increased efficiency, the perception of the organisation as family friendly, improved retention and the attraction of more talent.

You may feel that you have found a good opportunity for flexible working in your department, and want to take it further. You could discuss your ideas with your manager or write a short paper.

◆ Recap

Identify the main stages in the recruitment and selection process and consider the central role of the line manager

The recruitment and selection process typically comprises the following stages:

Planning	◆ Decide whether recruitment is necessary
	◆ Analyse the job
	◆ Write a job description, competency profile and person specification
Recruitment	◆ Decide on most appropriate application methods
	◆ Decide how to attract applicants
	◆ Market the job
Selection	◆ Sift and shortlist applications
	◆ Hold selection interviews and/or events
	◆ Make a decision and offer
	◆ Take up references
Induction	◆ Induct and train the new employee

Assess how the legal framework for recruitment and selection supports the promotion of equal opportunities and a diverse workforce

- The law encourages organisations to pursue the benefits of a diverse workforce. These benefits include greater empathy with customer groups, a wider range of ideas, improved morale and a larger talent pool from which to find scarce labour.

- Recruiters need to be fully aware of equal opportunities legislation and understand how discrimination can occur, both directly and indirectly, in the recruitment process.

Analyse the strengths and weaknesses of the recruitment and selection process in your organisation

- The process of and responsibilities for, recruitment and selection vary from one organisation to the next and are likely to be influenced by your HR policy. As the manager for the new recruit, it is beneficial for you to be involved in the process as much as possible.

Explore alternatives to external recruitment for addressing shortfalls in an organisation's pool of skills, knowledge and experience

- External recruitment is an expensive option. Alternatives include promotion from within, redeployment of another staff member, overtime working and flexible working practices.

- Flexible working is an umbrella term that describes employment practices which differ from a 'traditional', full-time, permanent, nine to five contract. Flexible working is becoming an important recruitment and retention tool.

▶▶ More @

The Department for Trade and Industry provides an excellent toolkit of case studies and advice for implementing flexible working practices at **www.dti.gov.uk/bestpractice/people/flexible-working.htm**

Tyson, S. and York, A. (2000) *Essentials of HRM*, **Butterworth-Heinemann**
A recommended textbook for people wanting a more detailed explanation and overview of how recruitment and selection fits into an organisation's framework for human resource management. It has a whole section dedicated to obtaining human resources.

Roberts, G. (1997) *Recruitment and Selection – A Competency Approach*, **CIPD**
This book presents a comprehensive overview of the whole process of recruitment and examines all the key techniques involved. It shows how they link in with wider HR practices, and how and where competencies can be used to best effect.

The Equal Opportunities Commission has produced a series of checklists for managers and supervisors aimed at promoting equality of opportunity in the workplace. One covers recruitment. **www.eoc.org.uk/EOCeng/dynpages/EqualityChecklist.asp**

Search the website of the **Chartered Institute of Personnel and Development** (www.cipd.co.uk) for checklists and resources on recruitment and selection, the legal framework and advice on flexible working practices. It also provides an annual survey that monitors trends in recruitment, selection and retention at **www.cipd.co.uk/subjects/recruitmen/general/recruitretnt04.htm**

2 Profiling the role

You need to get the right people in place to get the job done – people who will contribute fully to achieving your department's objectives and, consequently, those of the business. You may need someone who is a team player with creativity and flair. You may want them to bring new skills, be enthusiastic and be able to ease some of the pressures on you, as a manager.

People like this do exist, but the only way of recruiting them into your team is to know exactly what you want in terms of the job and the person. Knowing this provides a strong foundation from which you can build your recruitment and selection process.

In this theme, you explore how you can build a meaningful and realistic profile for a job role.

You will:

♦ Review a range of methods for analysing a job

♦ Identify the purpose of a job description and person specification

♦ Explore what is meant by recruiting on competence

Job analysis

Job analysis means adopting a method for establishing what is required to perform a job efficiently and effectively.

The factors highlighted in Figure 2.1 indicate that jobs are no longer static. External pressures force change and organisations and their people must adapt to survive. This means that what a person was employed to do two years ago may no longer be relevant. Therefore recruiting someone on that basis means you don't get the skills you actually need.

Job analysis helps you to assess your requirements for the future, rather than basing decisions on historic information. At its simplest, the information obtained can be used to amend information relating to the job, such as the job description and person specification. This ensures the recruitment process is based on current data, making it easier to identify the person with the necessary skills and abilities. Systematic job analysis is increasingly important as external factors force people and jobs to adapt to survive.

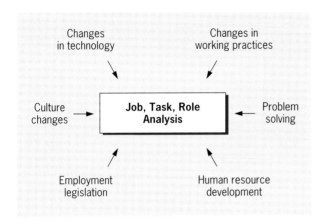

Figure 2.1 *Why job analysis is so important*

Source: *Pearn and Kandola* (1993)

Who to involve

Who you involve in a job analysis is largely dependent on how simple or complex the exercise is. At the very minimum it will be yourself and the jobholder. However, there is a strong case for involving others. For example, it can be useful to gain the perspective of your own manager who can see the job within the context of the organisation as a whole. It can also be helpful to include people who may be affected by the job, such as other parts of the business, customers or suppliers. It's useful to gain their views on what changes would help to improve the quality of service they receive.

If the job is technical or complex, you could also include others with expertise in the same or similar activities. If you have a human resource function, it should clearly be involved. Indeed, if you have an HR department, it is likely to take the lead as staff are trained in job analysis techniques.

What you need to find out

Job analysis is about finding out what the role is all about, and why it exists and how it contributes to the goals of the organisation. Therefore any analysis will need to identify:

- the purpose of the role
- the tasks and responsibilities that are required of the jobholder
- the skills, knowledge and abilities needed for effective performance
- the targets that are used to measure performance.

Job analysis methodology

Make sure any analysis you conduct is not influenced by your opinions of the jobholder as a person. The following information, based on the work of Pearn and Kandola (1993), provides an overview of the most common job analysis methods.

Observation. This is probably the most straightforward and easy-to-use technique. It involves recording everything the jobholder is doing as part of the job. It provides an overview of a job, but does not highlight the level of difficulty of the various tasks or the importance of each. It can be made more meaningful if the jobholder is also interviewed while performing the role. It works best for routine activities where the tasks can be seen in sequence, such as machine operation or on a production line.

Diaries and logs. This involves the jobholder recording what they do. This might happen at the end of a given time period or when they change from one activity to another. This method can be useful for jobs where the day-to-day activities are not easily observable, for example, in management. However, it can become subjective as the jobholder concentrates only on those areas of work that they consider to be important.

Job analysis interviews. This involves interviewing the jobholder, without a predetermined list of questions or checklist, thus bringing greater flexibility to the discussion. It can involve talking around the job description or bringing two jobholders together to talk about their work. It can be used for a variety of jobs and requires strong interviewing techniques on the part of the manager.

Critical incident technique. This concentrates on collecting information about critical incidents that are related to success and failure in a job. The incidents are recorded in relation to how the person handles certain situations and a composite picture is built up. The analysis can take place through keeping a log, completing a pro forma and/or interviews. It is useful for a range of jobs but can be time-consuming as many incidents must be recorded to obtain a full picture.

Repertory grid. Like critical incident analysis, this allows the identification of good and poor performance. It is generally undertaken with the manager or supervisor of people doing the same job, using a system of cards. The names of three people are written on cards, separated into two piles – one for good performers, one for poor. The supervisor then pulls out two good and one bad, and is asked to describe how the two good performers are similar and how they differ from the bad. The exercise is then repeated. This is a very flexible tool, but does require an enormous amount of data for it to work, and it's a highly skilled activity.

Checklist/inventories. This involves developing a list of tasks associated with a job and asking the jobholder to indicate which ones they perform and to rank them in order. While one checklist is needed for each job, it is a method that can be used for all types of jobs. It also produces some quantifiable data because of the ratings people provide.

In addition to the job analysis techniques outlined above, which can be developed and managed internally, there are a number of packages developed by commercial companies. For example, the Work Profiling System (WPS) is a structured technique developed by Saville and Holdsworth. It consists of three job analysis questionnaires relating to three categories of work: managerial/professional, service/administrative, and manual/technical.

The greater the need for change, the more sophisticated the analysis system will need to be.

Where analysis can take you
With 13,500 employees and 681 branches, Nationwide is the largest UK building society to have bucked the trend of the past decade and stayed mutual.

Following this decision, it developed a new business strategy in 1995 to improve levels of customer service and streamline services generally. It devolved more decision-making to line managers and introduced better controls. One-over-one reporting relationships were abolished and spans of control for managers were extended...

The job-family structure was developed after a detailed analysis of work. Five levels of decision-making were identified. Level one contains those roles where decision-making extends over a few days or weeks and the work is fairly well patterned. Level two is for technical and professional staff. Level three is the first level of management, and level four is for senior managers who are concerned with strategic direction, turning corporate strategies into action. Directors are level five.

Generic role definitions were then produced by staff groups setting out key accountabilities, and roles were allocated to levels within job families.

At level one, there are four job families: general services, specialist services, support services and customer services. At level two there are three job families: customer relations (the sales force), leading people (team managers) and specialist advice. There are only two job families at level three, professional development and leading implementation (the big operational roles). There is one family at levels four and five. Thus, there is a total of 11 job families.

A framework of six core capabilities was also developed, for career development planning, and potential identification purposes. A comprehensive job evaluation was carried out to validate this process.

Source: *Armstrong* (2000)

Activity 7
Conducting a job analysis

Objective

Use this activity to carry out a job analysis on your own role or another role within your department.

Task

1 Choose the job you are going to analyse. This can be your own job or someone else's in the department. If you decide to analyse someone else's job, make sure it is task-based. In other words, it is easy to see and understand what they do.

2 Decide which analysis method(s) you are going to use.

3 In analysing the job, you need to identify:

  ◆ the purpose of the role

  ◆ the tasks and responsibilities that are required of the jobholder

  ◆ the skills, knowledge and abilities needed for effective performance

  ◆ the targets that are used to measure performance.

4 Carry out the analysis and record your findings on the blank form below.

Job analysis

Job title: Method used:

Purpose of the job:

Tasks and responsibilities   *Skills, knowledge and abilities*   *Targets*

Feedback

What you probably found with that activity is the more straightforward the role, the simpler the method you could use.

The information you have generated can now form the basis of a recruitment campaign to attract suitable applicants. It can be used to develop the job description, using the tasks and responsibilities, and targets. It is also the basis for developing the person specification, using the information you've listed under skills, knowledge and abilities.

The job description and person specification

At the core of most recruitment and selection procedures are the job description and person specification. The job description states the purpose, responsibilities and conditions of the job. The person or employee specification outlines the abilities and qualities that would best fit the job.

Why these documents are important

The job description is at the heart of any recruitment you undertake. It is derived from a thorough job analysis and it specifies exactly what the job involves. It is therefore important in developing the person specification. It can also be used as the basis of advertising and be sent to applicants requiring further information.

If it is accurate, it presents a fair picture of what the job involves on a daily basis. This last point is important and can save you time and money. If potential applicants can identify whether they are capable of doing the job, then inappropriate people usually rule themselves out at an early stage.

The person specification is used as the basis of the selection process. It also goes some way to providing evidence that your selection process is fair. It can be used in marketing the role, makes shortlisting and selection easier, and helps to make the process objective. This is because all parties are clear about the qualities and abilities being sought.

Writing a job description

The job description describes the job and how it fits into the organisation. A good job description will include:

- job title
- location/department/areas of the business
- the grade of job, if relevant
- the overall purpose of the job
- the title of the person to whom the jobholder reports
- the title of any employees who report to the jobholder
- the main duties and responsibilities of the post, prioritised in some way, for example by order or by giving each a percentage weighting
- any other significant information, such as special working conditions
- the date of issue.

It is now common to group activities into key result areas and to indicate expected standards of performance in each area. This places greater emphasis on results, rather than inputs.

Checklist – writing a job description

- Check that it does not overstate the importance and scope of the role
- Make sure that there is no bias in terms of gender, age, marital status or disability
- Ensure sexist language has been avoided
- Make sure the language is clear and easily understood by someone from outside the organisation
- Check it doesn't include jargon, acronyms or abbreviations and use as few technical terms as possible
- Consider offering flexible working arrangements such as the possibility of a job-share
- Avoid including an age range as it is meaningless in determining past experience and you may eliminate the most capable candidate
- Make sure the audience it is aimed at can easily understand it.

Putting together a person specification

The person specification is derived from the job description. The factors you include in the person specification will be the criteria against which you judge candidates' suitability. Unrealistic criteria on a person specification may deter the most able candidate for the post.

The two most widely known formats for developing a person specification are Rodger's seven-point plan (1952) and Munro Fraser's five-fold grading (1954), which are shown in Table 2.1.

Rodger's seven-point plan	Fraser's five-fold grading
Physical make-up	Impact on others
Attainments	Qualifications or acquired knowledge
General intelligence	Innate abilities
Special aptitudes	Motivation
Interests	Adjustments or emotional balance
Disposition	
Circumstances	

Table 2.1 *Formats for developing a person specification*

Source: *Torrington and Hall* (1998)

Most of today's specifications are developed, in part, from these two early models, with some adjustments to take into account good equal opportunities practice. The most common format usually includes the following information:

◆ **skills** required such as planning, communication and teamworking

◆ **knowledge** requirements such as ability to work with computers, handle statistics, writing reports

◆ **experience** such as previous types of job and relevant interests

◆ **educational** qualifications, professional qualifications, technical skills

◆ **special requirements** such as shift work, a valid driving licence, physical demands of the job.

Bear in mind that experience gained away from work can be equally as valid as that gained in work.

Once the employee specification is drawn up, these factors are usually divided into essential and desirable. Essential are those criteria a candidate must possess to perform the job. Skills and qualifications are nearly always essential and will be the main things you use for shortlisting. Desirable are those that may allow a candidate to perform better in the role – the 'nice-to-haves'.

Checklist – putting together a person specification

When putting together a person specification, make sure it is:

♦ directly related to the job description

♦ ability-based in line with the requirements of the role

♦ realistic in terms of how the factors you choose contribute to job performance

♦ clearly defined

♦ measurable and/or observable

♦ agreed by everyone involved in the process

♦ weighted realistically in terms of essential and desirable qualities

♦ justifiable in terms of the criteria you have chosen.

Once the person specification is agreed it should not be changed and must be applied equally to all candidates.

Activity 8
Looking at job profiles

Objective

As a manager you need to be able to help develop appropriate and accurate job profiles. This activity will help you to comment on a job description and person specification and to make recommendations for change.

Task

1 Look at the following job description and person specification for a sales assistant.

Job description

Job title:	Sales executive
Location:	Working on the shop counter in a busy warehouse in Doncaster with three other executives
Job purpose:	To advise trade customers in the selection of bathroom fittings for the home. To sell, merchandise and arrange deliveries. To maximise sales
Reports:	None

Duties and responsibilities:

- Advise customers on fittings
- Keep the shop area tidy
- Organise delivery dates/times with warehouse supervisor
- Sell goods to the value of £150,000 each year
- Advise on payment methods
- Take payments correctly

- Proper use of equipment associated with payment – Visa, Mastercard and Maestro
- Maintain stock control system (computerised)
- Take part in stocktaking when required
- Take part in training when required
- Apply customer service skills

Salary: £11,500 per annum

Working conditions: Front of warehouse is a challenging work environment: it can be dirty and cold in the winter. The job entails working with a very challenging set of customers.

Person specification

Job title: Sales executive

	Essential	Desirable
Skills	◆ Customer service skills ◆ Patience ◆ Ability to work alone ◆ Planning and organising skills ◆ Ability to empathise with customers ◆ Interpersonal skills ◆ Sense of humour ◆ Willing and able to recommend improvements to processes	◆ Assertiveness ◆ Leadership ◆ Creative
Knowledge	◆ Computer skills ◆ Basic plumbing	◆ Knowledge of our system (Droneon II) ◆ Bathroom fitments
Experience	◆ One year in same or similar business ◆ Experience in a customer-facing role	◆ Minimum two years working for a competitor
Qualifications	◆ Maths Grade A at GCSE ◆ Computing Grade C at GCSE	◆ Maths A Level ◆ Plumbing qualification
Special requirements	◆ Clean driving licence ◆ Professional in manner and dress ◆ Vigorous, healthy and strong	◆ Available for overtime when need arises

2 Comment on what is good and bad about the job description and person specification above, and note down your recommendations for change.

Job description

Good points   *Bad points*

Recommendations for improvements

Person specification

Good points   *Bad points*

Recommendations for change

Feedback

Your comments may include some of the following points:

Job description

Good points
It is detailed and covers most of the essential information of a good job description.

You get a clear impression of what it would be like to do the job in that work environment through the location, job purpose and working conditions.

Bad points and improvements
The job title is a little too impressive for the role – this is an assistant, not an executive.

It does not say to whom the person reports – this needs to be added.

The duties and responsibilities seem to be in a random order and need to be prioritised. For example, selling goods to the value of £150,000 should probably be at the top. In fact, this is actually a standard of performance and would deserve a separate section.

Some of the duties are rather vague, for example 'keep the shop area tidy' should have the required standard added.

Some of the duties are very high level, for example 'advise customers on fittings', while others are very detailed, for example the reference to equipment associated with payment which is really part of taking payments and could be omitted.

The occasional duties of stocktaking and training should be put at the end of the list.

The statement about working with challenging customers under the working conditions heading could be seen negatively, unless it is explained in more detail.

Person specification

Good points
Again, this goes into quite a lot of detail.

It covers the main categories of skills, knowledge, experience, qualifications and special requirements.

It divides criteria into essential and desirable.

Bad points and improvements
It seems to be asking for someone who is overqualified: is a top grade maths qualification really necessary for the job?

A lot of skills are listed, and the essential requirement, customer service skills, needs further explanation. Also, it is unlikely that a sales assistant would need to display leadership or even creativity.

Some of the criteria are questionable. For example, why is a clean driving licence essential? What is meant by professional manner and dress – particularly bearing in mind the job is in a warehouse?

One of the worst aspects is that the specification could be discriminatory. For example, it is asking for qualifications only young people will have (GCSEs) and it is asking for the person to be vigorous and strong.

Using competence

Increasingly organisations are using the outputs from job analysis to create competence frameworks that capture the knowledge and skills that will result in the requisite level of job performance. Progressively job descriptions and person specifications are being built around competence frameworks.

Competence can be defined as:

> ...an underlying characteristic of a person which results in effective and/or superior performance in a job.
>
> Source: *Boyatzis* (1982)

> ...the ability to perform the activities within an occupational area to the levels of performance expected in employment.
>
> Source: *Training Commission* (1988)

As the authors point out, the two definitions are slightly different but that:

> ...the concept of competence integrates knowledge and skills which are assessed via performance.
>
> Source: *Beardwell and Holden* (1997)

Why the competence route?

It is generally believed that this offers an organisation greater flexibility in recruitment. This is because statements of competence, or competencies, are commonly developed for a particular occupation, such as management, rather than a specific job. This gives more flexibility because specific jobs may change rapidly, but this is less likely to happen with 'families' of jobs.

Competence takes into account the changing structures of an organisation. For example, where managing a cross-functional team becomes a requirement, the manager can still be assessed against the competencies for the role. With a job description, this would be more difficult as it is a specific list of duties and responsibilities.

At selection stage, competencies also provide a framework against which people can provide evidence of competence, in whatever setting – rather than a checklist of 'can and can't do'. It could be argued it is a fairer way for people to show potential for the future, as well as their capacity to undertake a particular job.

....competencies mean that it is not only possible to select against them, but to predict the workplace behaviours of the candidate and monitor performance against them, aligning performance management and training programmes to support and enhance optimum performance. Thus the creation of a competency-based specification provides clear, quantifiable measurements of people; it allows the principles of total quality management to be applied to the management of human resources.

Source: *Roberts* (1997)

Identifying key competencies

You should not attempt to develop competencies without help. You may be able to conduct an analysis of one job, but to analyse for competence within a group of jobs is a bigger task altogether.

Critical incident analysis and the repertory grid technique are both helpful in identifying competencies because they are both ways of differentiating good from poor performance. However, if you are considering this route, expert help is essential. It is a time-consuming, challenging task and is usually part of a wider cultural change in terms of how an organisation manages its human resource. It is also vitally important that any move towards a competency framework is supported by strong performance management systems. Therefore appraisal, objective setting, development planning, coaching and training must be in place to underpin any change. A competency framework must be underpinned by a strong system of performance management.

Competencies at the FCO

The 10 competencies listed here were developed for the recruits into the Foreign and Commonwealth Office for grade DS9. This is the 'main stream' entry point for employees based in London and in offices overseas involved in consular, management, commercial and immigration work.

- ◆ organising your own work
- ◆ managing staff and resources
- ◆ withstanding rigours of overseas life
- ◆ handling conflicting priorities
- ◆ mixing easily with other people
- ◆ making sense of complex information
- ◆ writing critical/sensitive documents
- ◆ using computers and IT
- ◆ making good decisions quickly
- ◆ practical problem solving.

Source: *Lee et al.* (1998)

Breaking it down further

Competencies alone are not enough to assess suitability for recruitment. A common route is to determine the features of a good performer against each competency, as Table 2.2 indicates.

Competency	Behavioural indicator
Communication skills	Strong writing and oral skills, ability to express thoughts clearly
	Seeks out and develops productive working relationships
	Listens with empathy, responds diplomatically
Flexibility	Open and receptive to new ideas
	Ability to adapt to changing priorities, situations and demands
	Willingness to learn new skills
Initiative	Anticipates needs and takes action without waiting to be told
	Suggests ways of being more efficient
	Asks questions and offers new ideas

Table 2.2 *Sample competencies for administrative and accounts assistants at Cornell University*   Source: *Cornell University* (1999)

However, the following points are interesting from Jeff Standridge, organisational development leader at Acxiom Corporation in Little Rock, Arkansas:

> Most companies cluster a group of related skills together and call it a competency. A communication competency, for example, would probably include common skills like writing, speaking and making presentations. To change those (communication competencies) to behaviour statements upon which our job roles and competency models are based, you might say the person actively listens, builds trust and adapts his style and tactics to fit the audience. These behaviours won't change, even as the means of executing them evolve with technology.
>
> To define job roles, the company examined the successful behaviours of its good performers.
>
> Standridge says, 'When we asked a panel "What makes this employee a successful software developer?" the first answer would be, "Well he knows Java and C++ etc"...
>
> When we asked "If Java becomes obsolete in five years, will this person no longer be successful" the panel responded "Oh no, he'll update his skills and become great in the new language."'

The employee's strength was not just in his specific skills but in his ability to learn.

Standridge adds, 'What we did was move beyond skills to behaviourally anchored competencies like self-directed learning.'

Source: *Joinson* (2001)

Activity 9
The use of competencies

Objective

This activity will help you to consider the competencies that might be relevant to a job within your department.

Task

1 Choose a job role to examine. It could be your job or another job in your department. If the job is done by another person, and you want to talk to that person about the job, then make sure the person understands what you are doing and why.

2 If possible, look at the job description and person specification for the job — think about what the job involves and what the person doing the job actually does.

3 Identify the key competencies for this job. Choose the five or six main ones. The following list of example competencies will help you to get started, but there are many more possibilities.

4 Use the blank chart opposite to write down each competency and then list the types of behaviour that might show this competency is being achieved. Keep this to a maximum of four types for each one. See below for an example of the types of behaviour for the competency, communication.

Example competencies

Communication	Creativity and innovation
Leadership	Resilience
Managing others	Flexibility
Planning and organising	Results orientated
Customer focus	Judgement

Example competency and types of behaviour

Competency	Behavioural indicators
Communication	Writes in a clear and concise manner, using appropriate grammar, language and style
	Speaks in a compelling manner to individuals and groups
	Uses the most appropriate communication mechanism in a given situation
	Listens with empathy to the views and opinions of others

Possible competencies for the role of ....

Competency	Behavioural indicators

Feedback

The contents of your list will depend on which role you have chosen. It may be useful to check with the jobholder that they agree with your findings. Below is an example against which you can cross-check your indicators for leadership.

Competency	Behavioural indicators
Leadership	Is focused on what needs to be done to achieve organisational goals
	Motivates others in order to achieve results
	Empowers and develops others
	Acts as ambassador and spokesperson for the team

◆ Recap

Review a range of methods for analysing a job

◆ Job analysis details the criteria for successful job performance. Typically, it focuses on identifying tasks and responsibilities, knowledge and skill requirements, and the targets used to measure performance.

◆ Observation of performance, interviews with jobholders as well as more specialist techniques like the repertory grid and critical incident analysis can be used to analyse a job.

Identify the purpose of a job description and person specification

◆ All recruitment should start with a job description and a person specification that documents the necessary and desirable criteria that will be used as the basis of the selection process.

◆ These should be written using language that is clear and accurate to ensure equity in the selection process and to enable potential applicants to self-assess whether they are capable of doing the job.

Explore what is meant by recruiting on competence

◆ Competence frameworks typically express either the behavioural characteristics or the job outputs required for superior performance in a role. Increasingly, they form the basis for the job description and person specification.

♦ Application forms, interview questions and testing procedures can all be designed to require the candidate to demonstrate evidence of their competence against the framework.

 **More @**

Roberts, G. (1997) *Recruitment and Selection – A Competency Approach*, **CIPD**
This book presents a comprehensive overview of the whole process of recruitment and selection, including job analysis, from a competency perspective.

The SHL Group, a leader in selection practices, publishes guidelines for best practice in the use of job analysis techniques at **www.shlgroup.com/uk/litigation/BestPractice/BestPractice_JobAnalysis.pdf**

Tyson, S. and York, A. (2000) *Essentials of HRM*, **Butterworth-Heinemann**
Chapter 7 explores job analysis and defining effective performance.

3 Recruitment strategies

Once you know what type of person you want, you need to find them and persuade them to apply – this is your recruitment strategy. The ultimate aim of any recruitment strategy is to attract good-quality applicants by the most objective, cost-effective and swift means possible.

You'll start your work in this theme by considering how you can gather information about potential applicants. There are two commonly used options: the CV and the application form.

You'll then go on to explore the various approaches for marketing job vacancies. Your aim is to reach a broad and diverse range of candidates who meet your selection criteria. In labour markets where there are skill shortages, this might prove particularly difficult. You'll consider how IT is being used alongside traditional methods of recruitment to reach a wider pool of applicants.

Your objectives for this theme are to:

♦ Review the relative merits of using application forms and CVs to capture candidate data

♦ Explore types of recruitment advertising for attracting a diverse range of candidates

♦ Identify the features of a good recruitment advertisement

♦ Consider how IT is being used to streamline the recruitment process

♦ Identify alternative approaches to advertising for reaching potential candidates.

Application form versus CV

The benefits of an application form

An application form provides an easy method for examining the suitability of different candidates for the post on offer. This is because everyone is required to provide similar information, making a like-for-like comparison easier.

If you ask people to send their CV, you could say they have a better opportunity to demonstrate their suitability for the post. On the other hand, it makes it more difficult to compare people. Each CV may provide very different information and when dozens have to be sifted through, it is quite possible to apply inconsistent criteria and miss the most suitable candidate.

Another problem with a CV is that it's rarely developed for the job you're offering, so you may receive information that is of no relevance at all. On a CV, people tend to tell you what they want you to hear, rather than what you need to know. Many firms now offer CV writing services, therefore a well-structured CV may have been developed by someone paid for the task, giving a very positive image which may flatter the individual.

While it may initially seem like an administrative burden to send out application forms, it can save time in the long run. You can use the opportunity to send an information pack with the application form. For example, you can send further information about the post, the oganisation, the job description and person specification. These will all help candidates assess their own suitability for the job in question and some will choose not to take their application further on the basis of information you provide.

This means the forms you receive back are of a good quality as people are beginning the process of selection for you.

Applying online

An increasing number of employers now offer online options to applicants. Some of these are simply application forms that you download and print out but others provide forms for completion online.

One of the biggest advantages of applying electronically is that the distractions of handwriting and paper quality are removed. The focus is on the content. Administration is also streamlined – there is no need to post out application forms and completed applications can be circulated easily in electronic form.

Equal opportunities implications

A number of equal opportunities implications surround the use of CVs and application forms.

Application forms are recognised as good equal opportunities practice as they make it easier to match the information provided with the person specification. A structured application form makes it easier to compare applicants with the person specification for the role.

Some very good candidates can be put off if you ask for a CV. They may have no experience of putting one together and may not have the money to have one professionally produced.

The application form can be structured in such a way that irrelevant information is not requested. For example, information such as age, marital status and children are irrelevant to someone's ability to do the job. On a CV, applicants may provide this sort of detail and this may influence some people involved in shortlisting.

Details on an application form

The following details can be requested on an application form:

◆ job applied for

◆ name, address, telephone number (home and work)

◆ previous employment – name and address of employer, job title, dates position held, main duties/responsibilities, salary

◆ education, qualifications gained plus dates

◆ other relevant skills, experience, interests

◆ name and address of two referees.

You need to make sure:

◆ the form is professionally produced – giving a positive image of the organisation

◆ the form is error-free and jargon-free

◆ there is sufficient space for people to write their responses

◆ the form clearly states what information is required

◆ all relevant aspects of the job can be covered

◆ it does not contain anything that might be discriminatory or offensive

◆ there is space to sign and date the form.

A different approach – biodata

Biodata is a variation of the traditional application form. It consists of a series of multiple-choice questions. Some require a factual answer, while others are about preferences, values and attitudes. Candidates' responses are compared with the ideal responses for the job.

While still not widely used, biodata does have its uses where competencies are being used, as the answers given can be compared to what differentiates good from poor performance. It is also useful when a number of posts are available at the same level.

Biodata is also a relatively good indicator of job performance, scoring 0.40 on a scale where 1.0 is perfect prediction, but where unstructured interviews score only 0.31 and references only 0.13.

Biodata in practice

A large retailer in the UK receives huge numbers of applications from graduates each year. Working with biodata analysis, the application forms are screened in a purely mechanical way, with points being scored for certain criteria, before initial shortlists are drawn up. In this way the company avoids the need to spend expensive executive time in scrutinising all the application forms. This is a very workable strategy when you have a very large number of applicants.

Source: *Torrington and Hall* (1998)

Looking at the role

In general it is better to use an application form because consistent information is provided which can reduce the time for shortlisting. It is also particularly useful when the job is fairly standardised and you expect a large number of applicants.

It's common practice to request a CV for management or technical posts as it allows an individual to express their suitability for a post more fully. In cases such as this, a compromise is to issue an application form and ask applicants to provide additional information about their suitability on a separate sheet.

Activity 10
Approaches to recruitment

Objective

Use this activity to examine your own recruitment methods.

Case study

Read the following case study.

The way we used to do things round here

I'm responsible for recruiting most of the staff in the department – everyone from the cleaners up to the designers. We used to have a two-tier system. For what we call the functional roles, people filled in an application form and had an interview. On the creative side, people sent in their CV and had an interview. It seemed a bit low level to ask graduates and postgraduates to fill in an application form. We wanted creative people so we wanted to see creative applications.

Oh boy we got them! CVs in every shape and form you could imagine. In fact they were so creative it was impossible to compare people. It took ages to work through them all.

When we analysed what was happening we found that too big a percentage of our graduates just weren't staying with us. I know they're in demand and are likely to change jobs frequently, but not so many within the first 12 months for goodness' sake!

So we had a shake-up of the whole system. We developed application forms for all these creative jobs, which wasn't too hard as many of them are similar. Instead of relying on interview alone, we now use a type of assessment centre. We do use some bought-in tests, but it's mainly to do with looking at how people deal with situations at work – role-plays and simulations.

We're now more confident that we are bringing in the right people to assess in the first place. And also that the two-day assessment is fairer on both sides – we have a good chance of assessing them properly and they can see if we're really the type of business they want to work for.

It's working – the number of graduates leaving in the first 12 months is down by 75 per cent.

Task

In light of the information you have read, review your own department's recruitment methods and make six recommendations for change. Provide a brief justification for each one.

Recruitment methods in my department:

Recommendations for change and why:

Feedback

The type of changes you may have noted down could be among the following examples:

- Use application forms rather than requesting CVs – you receive the information that you need, it makes comparison between applicants easier and it saves time.

- Ask applicants for a 500-word explanation of why they are suited to the job – this lets people show their creativity, and highlights how much relevant experience they have.

- If requesting a CV, state on the job advertisement exactly what you expect to see – this makes it easier to compare like with like, and may cut down on the detail.

- Review the interview process thoroughly – to check that interviews are achieving the desired result and that everyone is fully trained and briefed in what is expected of them.

- Introduce some form of testing rather than just using an interview – this gives people a fairer chance of displaying their skills.

- Look at the feasibility of setting up assessment centres for some jobs – it seems that they are a good predictor of job performance if developed and administered properly.

Advertising a vacancy

Once you've decided how you want people to apply, you're ready to advertise your post. Advertising your vacancy in the press is still recognised as one of the best methods for reaching your target audience. However, there are a number of choices you must make, depending on time, the job you are marketing, the possible size of your target market and, importantly, the budget you have available.

Many organisations still use press advertising extensively, despite the costs involved. It is a tried and tested option and, if framed correctly, the advert can provide a positive image of your organisation. This is likely to be seen by a wider audience than just the people who may apply to you. In other words, it's another marketing vehicle for your organisation.

Another plus point is that if you are new to recruitment advertising, specialist agencies can provide expert help. Some publications prepare copy themselves, which is helpful if you're not confident enough to have a go yourself. However, in either case, you will need to ensure copy complies with good equal opportunities practice.

Good equal opportunities practice in recruitment advertising

- Avoid specifying age or requesting qualifications that only the young may have, such as GCSEs or GNVQs

- Avoid using terms such as 'dynamic', 'young', 'energetic', which again imply the suitability of young people

- Avoid being gender specific in job titles and refer to potential candidates as 'he/she' or 'they'

- Avoid photographs that show a particular type of applicant, for example showing a picture of all-male, all-white, twenty-something employees suggests that you are looking for this type of person

- Avoid symbols or visuals that represent strength and power – usually associated with a male, for example certain types of animals such as tigers and lions

- Avoid overstating the job – you may get somebody who is highly qualified but who is not the most suitable person for the job

- The job description and person specification should always be the basis of a recruitment advertisement.

What are your choices?

In terms of press advertising, there are four main choices.

The national press – this is usually in the 'quality' press such *The Times*, *The Telegraph* and *The Guardian* in the UK. These papers tend to feature different types of jobs on different days.

Local press – often the best choice for non-specialist jobs, as they will reach a wide audience if you are looking for local labour. Some city-based papers have a huge circulation, such as the *Yorkshire Post*, *Manchester Evening News* and *London Evening Standard*. Some local papers are part of a group of publications and may offer reduced rates in their sister papers.

Trade press – if you have a specialised post to fill, this may be your best option. Be careful, because some publications are subscription only. Some companies may only subscribe to one copy and it may take time to filter down to your target group.

Minority press – this is a useful method if you are trying to attract applicants from particular ethnic groups, usually in the local area.

Table 3.1 highlights the advantages and disadvantages of various forms of press advertising.

Location	Advantages	Disadvantages
National press	Good for senior posts or those where skills are scarce Will reach a national audience	Costly – based on size of advert and location on the page
Local press	Good for all but senior and highly specialised posts Relatively inexpensive	May not look as professional as advertising in the nationals Can miss some able applicants who may live out of area
Trade press	Good for specialised and technical posts Usually a mid-priced option	Be wary of claims for large readership figures which may not be the same as publications sold
Minority press	Will clearly target certain sectors of the population Can be an inexpensive option	May miss a wider audience Could be additional costs involved if the advert needs translating

Table 3.1 *Press advertising*

Getting the best from the press
Before advertising in the press, make sure you know the following:

♦ the paper's circulation figures and/or readership profile

♦ the paper's geographical coverage

♦ the best day to advertise for the post you have available

♦ on which page of the publication your advert will appear

♦ where your advert will appear on the page and the cost of premium placements

- the costs involved – and what you get for your money in terms of size and location
- what assistance you can expect in preparing copy – and at what cost
- whether the journal has a relationship with any advertising agencies where you might expect a reduced rate
- what the copy deadlines are.

Working with an agency

Deciding whether to work with an advertising agency will depend on a range of factors such as the level of job you are advertising, your budget and your personal level of experience in recruitment advertising.

Using an agency can seem an expensive option but may be cost-effective in the long term. For example, the agency may be able to negotiate discounts for space. Its experience of developing and placing professional advertisements may be hard to match within your organisation. In addition, the brief you provide may help you to clarify your own thoughts about what you want.

Putting together a recruitment advert

Whether working with an agency or working alone, preparation is the key to successful recruitment advertising. The advert must appear in the right place at the right time, contain all the necessary information and have an appearance that is appropriate to the job.

There are three areas to consider when designing an advertisement for the press. They are size, style and content.

Size

The size will control the number of words you have available and the format of the headline you use.

The size will be affected by the following factors:

- your budget versus the cost of space in the publication
- the seniority of the post or number of posts available
- the speciality of the post on offer
- the importance of the post to the organisation
- the known scarcity of quality candidates to fill the post
- the size of other adverts competing for similar candidates.

Style

The style is to do with the way the advert looks on the page. It consists of these elements:

Layout. Use the border of the advert to draw the reader into it. Avoid using a small type size to fit in more words – it will only looked cramped. Easy-to-read copy with plenty of white space is more appealing, even if it includes less detail.

Typeface. Choose a common typeface and use upper and lower case as it's easier to read. If you have corporate guidelines on typeface and design, then use them as it helps promote the right image.

Visuals. These are nice to have but can be expensive. So if your budget is limited, a larger advertisement is probably better than one that's elaborate but smaller. However, visuals that are an integral part of your organisation's image, such as logos, should be included. If using visuals in press advertising, make sure they comply with good equal opportunities practice.

Colour. As with visuals, colour can be an unnecessary expense. However, you may want to consider a small area of single colour that can attract the reader's eye if everything else on the page is in black and white.

Content

The content of your advertisement is the main element in attracting suitable applicants.

The following details are all relevant:

◆ name of the organisation

◆ location, size and brief details about the organisation

◆ job title and basic information based on the job description

◆ job tenure, for example length of contract

◆ skills and qualities needed, based on the person specification

◆ any essential qualifications

◆ salary and other benefits

◆ hours and any flexible working on offer

◆ how, where and to whom to apply

◆ the closing date

◆ telephone number plus fax or e-mail address to request an application form and further details.

A checklist of points to bear in mind when preparing a recruitment advert is provided in Table 3.2.

Do...	Don't...
Use the organisation's name, the job, the location and salary in the heading	Exaggerate the job or the organisation's track-record
Include any organisational successes, e.g. recent growth	Use generalised statements about the responsibilities of the job
Be specific about salary	Include criteria that applicants do not need to meet to make the job sound more attractive
Highlight benefits that may attract applicants, especially if the salary is not overly attractive	
State what development opportunities are on offer	Use words that make the job more interesting, such as 'go-ahead' or 'dynamic' – they are meaningless and can deter some applicants

Table 3.2 *Dos and don'ts of recruitment advertising*

Check that all details in the advert are accurate before submitting it to the press. Also speak to a specialist or a lawyer to ensure the advert complies with the law. Remember it is illegal to advertise a position in such a way that it either directly or indirectly discriminates on the grounds of gender, race or disability and it is not good practice to discriminate on the grounds of age.

Using the Internet

The Internet is an increasingly popular way of recruiting staff because it is quick and relatively easy. Organisations use both their own websites and those of the growing number of online job sites like www.monster.co.uk and www.fish4jobs.co.uk. Online job sites use technology to offer three main benefits to employers:

♦ the option to post a job on the job board

♦ screening and assessment of applicants against pre-set criteria

♦ access to a database of CVs from potential applicants already registered with the agency.

The CIPD *Recruitment, retention and turnover survey 2004* reported that almost 40% of employers use a job board to post vacancies.

Activity 11
Web-based recruitment advertising

Objective

This activity will help you to consider the advantages and disadvantages of web-based recruitment advertising.

Case study

Read the following extract from an article that appeared in *The Sunday Times*.

Using the web to catch graduates

Chris Gilchrist of GTI, a careers publishing company whose informative website Doctorjob.com is aimed at graduates, believes market pressures will force (employers) to look further afield. This means that it is becoming more important to refine their methods of identifying the right people.

Just as Asda uses its website to discourage the faint-hearted, others include some form of discreet screening. IBM gets candidates to take the IBM Challenge, which involves running a space station using IBM Think Pads. It gives the company an insight into candidates' communication, analytical and team-working skills – all the characteristics most sought by employers.

Hewens (Elaine Hewens of TMP Worldwide) believes firms should change their recruitment tactics. 'What you can do with websites is growing all the time,' she says. 'The milk-round is too wasteful. When you are looking for people with particular skills, there are much cheaper ways of doing it.'

The average graduate employer handles about 4,000 applications a year, according to the Association of Graduate Recruiters. Processing these is expensive. The task has to be managed carefully to avoid waste and to keep costs-per-hire under control.

What surprises Hewens is the large number of companies yet to adapt to what amounts to a revolution in recruitment. 'It has to fit in with the business's other objectives,' she says. 'The organisation that takes an ad hoc approach won't recruit.'

'The revolution is far from over. Text messaging on mobile phones could be one of the cheapest ways of contacting people and seems certain to become the next development in recruitment.'

Source: *Eglin* (2001)

Task

1 Make notes on what you see as the advantages and disadvantages of web-based recruitment over other forms, such as press advertising and using headhunters. Use the extract above and your own background knowledge to help you.

Advantages	Disadvantages

Feedback

You could have included some or all of these points in your answer:

Advantages

- ◆ It can be relatively inexpensive if you already have a website
- ◆ It is certainly less expensive than, for example, the milk-round, for graduate recruitment
- ◆ It can be designed in an original and eye-catching way
- ◆ It can be targeted at particular groups of workers, such as graduates
- ◆ Pre-screening can be built into it
- ◆ It shows your organisation as technologically aware and up-to-date
- ◆ Can potentially reach a worldwide audience
- ◆ Use of the Internet is growing, particularly among young job hunters.

Disadvantages

◆ It can be expensive if you are using a web company to advertise, and you may have less control over content

◆ Potential recruits may not visit your website

◆ Not all potential recruits may have access to the Internet, therefore it's probably not suitable for low-level jobs

◆ It is difficult to target specific people in the way that head hunters would

◆ It is difficult to monitor the quality of people visiting the site.

Alternative methods of recruitment

While the traditional route of attracting applicants for a vacant post is through press advertising, there are alternative approaches. Some of these can be arranged in-house, while others involve drawing on external specialists.

External organisations

If you are thinking about using external specialists, take time to fully examine what is available.

Employment agencies

Employment agencies generally hold a register of job seekers. They tend to specialise in jobs that are relatively low level and common across organisations, such as administrative staff, drivers or warehouse operatives. For a fee they will match your needs with people registered with them and will operate to fill vacancies quickly.

Recruitment consultancies

These organisations tend to specialise in management or sales posts. They generally have named individuals on their lists who may be either employed or unemployed. A large recruitment consultancy can draw on a national database or have links with other consultancies in different geographical areas.

You will need to manage any consultancy relationship and brief consultants very carefully. It's also important to ensure they match the person to your job, rather than the other way round, otherwise you could end up with an unsuitable employee.

Outplacement consultancies

These are organisations dealing specifically with people who have been made redundant, often from managerial and professional roles. Costs are relatively low and the calibre of people can be high. In addition, the consultant is likely to know the individual well as they work closely through a redundancy process.

Search consultancies

These are often referred to as 'head hunters' and are the most expensive option because they will look for suitable candidates currently working in other organisations. If you're considering head hunters, make sure the consultants understand your line of business and the type of employee you are looking for.

Questions to ask an external agency

'What would you see as a successful outcome?'

'What level of involvement do you have in the process?'

'How do you attract candidates for an organisation/opening like ours?'

'How much do you know about our business?'

'Who will work on our behalf and what is their experience?'

'How much time will this person devote to our search?'

'What other organisations are you working for at present?'

'Who do we speak to if our relationship appears not to be working?'

'What do you do to ensure good equal opportunities practices are incorporated into your work?'

'Can I have references from other organisations you have worked for?'

'How much is it going to cost and how are fees charged, for example by the hour or per project?'

Going it alone

You could always try to find suitable applicants yourself.

Job centres are still widely used for recruiting into low- skill, low-paid jobs. You provide the specific job details and the centre will make people aware that the job exists. However, they don't actively promote your business, so the information you provide must be carefully framed.

Local commercial radio is useful if recruiting for a number of positions at a semi-skilled or unskilled level. It is very different from press advertising and you will need to hire a scriptwriter to put your advert together.

Building long-term links with the local community is a good way of developing a future source of recruitment. This can be in local schools or colleges, through sponsorship or by taking people on work experience. Holding open days or giving talks to local community groups can attract people who may never have considered your organisation before.

Asda's raw recruits

Promising 'scenes of nudity, immense challenges and early responsibility which some people may find disturbing' Asda's graduate recruitment website includes pages with such titles as 'In the raw' and 'Leaving nothing to the imagination'. It also encourages applicants to send off for a video entitled 'The naked truth'.

It's an in-your-face approach spiced with humour – applicants who fail the filter quiz are redirected to the Sainsbury's website – carefully aimed at its target audience of graduates.

A successful recruitment campaign must always have the candidate in mind, according to Andrea Vowles, graduate resourcing manager at Asda, which was one of the first companies to recruit graduates on the Internet.

'The website must be designed to be interesting and fun to read' she says. 'We make the process interactive by including a quiz and video, but the most important rule is to have a simple application process. On some company websites it takes 45 minutes to complete the application, and no one can be bothered with that.'

Asda is recruiting 65 graduates this year and expects its offbeat approach to generate 2,000 applications.

Source: *Finn* (2000)

Finally, **internal marketing** is useful as part of a wider recruitment process. Full details of the post should be made available through notice boards, newsletters or the organisation's magazine or Intranet. Candidates are then assessed on exactly the same basis as those applying from outside. However, avoid relying on word-of-mouth advertising as this goes against good equal opportunities practice. Relying on word-of-mouth advertising can have the effect of cloning the workforce and reducing its creativity.

Your own organisation's website can be a useful (and free) vehicle to publicise your vacancy, particularly if the organisation has a high profile. It also has the added advantage that visitors to the website may be predisposed to working for you.

Activity 12
Advertising

Objectives

Use this activity to:

◆ assess the effectiveness of a recruitment advertisement

◆ identify where you might advertise for a selection of different types of job.

Task

1   Look at the following advertisement from Ealing, Hammersmith and Fulham NHS Trust and answer the question that follows.

Ealing, Hammersmith and Fulham NHS
Mental Health NHS Trust

Biomedical Engineer

Reference Number: OR51

**Salary – up to £25,000
depending on experience**

A vacancy exists in the Estates Services Department for a biomedical engineer. The work involves repair, calibration, safety and performance testing on a wide range of medical equipment in use by both Ealing and EHF NHS Trusts.

Applicants should be qualified to degree level in electronics engineering with a minium of 3 years experience in medical equipment maintenance.

Closing date for receipt of applications: 14th April 2001

For an application form and job description please contact the *Personnel Department at EHF Mental Health Trust, Uxbridge Road, Southall, UB1 3EU or telephone 020 8354 8090.*

Please quote relevant reference number.

Committed to Equal Opportunities

POSITIVE ABOUT DISABLED PEOPLE

Source: *The Telegraph* (2001)

What factors make the advertisement an effective recruitment advertisement?

2 What recruitment method(s) might you consider for the following jobs?

a) A new managing director for a 55-strong engineering company.

b) Six individuals who will form a sales team for a new area office.

c) Telesales staff for a new call centre in a major city.

d) Production line workers for a food manufacturer.

3 If you were responsible for choosing a newspaper in which to advertise a post, what would you want to find out in order to make your choice?

Make a checklist of points below:

- ◆
- ◆

- ◆
- ◆

- ◆
- ◆

- ◆
- ◆

Feedback

You may have noted some of the following points:

1 The advertisement has the following good features:

- ◆ It clearly states the organisation, position and salary in the headline, (although it is likely that this is the maximum salary on offer as it states 'dependent on experience')
- ◆ It provides an overview of what the job involves
- ◆ It states what qualifications and experience are required – assuming there is a valid reason for needing three years' experience
- ◆ It states where and how to apply – by application form
- ◆ The closing date is clear
- ◆ It includes the Trust's commitment to equal opportunities and the 'positive about disabled people' symbol
- ◆ The language is clear and jargon-free.

You may also have suggested that there is not much white space, although it is sufficient to make the advertisement easy to read.

2 You may have suggested the following recruitment methods.

(a) A new managing director might be found through advertising in the quality press such as *The Times* or *The Telegraph*. If suitable people are likely to be in short supply, then head hunting might be an option.

(b) Again, national advertising might be useful. Recruitment consultants could also be of help. It may also be worth asking others on the sales team if they know of anyone suitable.

(c) Local advertising, either in the paper or on local radio, is likely to be your best option as you're probably looking for local people.

(d) In the case of production workers, jobcentres are probably a good starting point, assuming it is unskilled or semi-skilled employees you require.

3 You may have suggested the following points:

◆ circulation figures and/or readership profile

◆ geographical coverage

◆ the best day to advertise

◆ on what page of the publication your advertisement will appear

◆ the costs for different sized advertisements and different locations

◆ the assistance you can expect in preparing copy, and the cost

◆ whether the newspaper has a relationship with any advertising agencies where you might expect a reduced rate

◆ what the copy deadlines are.

◆ Recap

Review the relative merits of using application forms and CVs to capture candidate data

◆ An application form captures a consistent set of information about each applicant, making comparison and shortlisting easier and fairer.

◆ Applicants have more freedom to express themselves in a CV and it's acceptable and common to request them for management and professional positions.

Explore types of recruitment advertising for attracting a diverse range of candidates

◆ Local, national, trade and minority press are widely used for recruitment advertising. Circulation figures, readership profile and geographical coverage of a publication help to indicate its suitability.

◆ The Internet is frequently used alongside or in place of press advertising.

Identify the features of a good recruitment advertisement

◆ Advertisements should describe the job accurately and should state:

  – title and requirements of the job

  – necessary and desirable criteria for job applicants

  – name, size and activities of the organisation

  – job location

  – reward package

  – job tenure, for example length of contract

  – the application procedure.

◆ Advertisements should be designed to appeal to all sections of the community by using positive visual images and appropriate wording.

Consider how IT is being used to streamline the recruitment process

◆ The Internet is helping to streamline administration associated with the recruitment process by enabling applicants to apply for jobs online.

◆ A growing number of job websites enable employers to post adverts for jobs and to search a database of CVs from people already registered with the site.

Identify alternatives approaches to advertising for reaching potential candidates

◆ Options include using specialist external agencies, such as employment agencies or head hunters, or promoting the vacancy internally.

 **More @**

Roberts, G. (1997) *Recruitment and Selection – A Competency Approach*, CIPD

This book presents a comprehensive overview of the whole process of recruitment and selection including recruitment techniques.

The Chartered Institute of Personnel and Development (CIPD) publishes a checklist for recruiting on the Internet at **www.cipd.co.uk/subjects/recruitmen/onlnrcruit/webrecruit.htm**. It also publishes an annual survey monitoring trends in recruitment at **www.cipd.co.uk/subjects/recruitmen/general/ recruitretnt04.htm**

4   The selection process

The selection process is becoming increasingly sophisticated. Although the traditional interview remains at the heart of the process, employers are making more use of testing techniques to sit alongside the interview and improve the reliability of the selection decision.

Figure 4.1 highlights the match between different selection methods and eventual job performance. What it shows is that some tests and assessment centres offer a 'far better than chance' prediction of performance on the job whereas an unstructured interview, on its own, is a relatively poor predictor of performance. For the manager, the lesson seems to be that the more variety you can bring to selection methods, the greater your chance of getting it right.

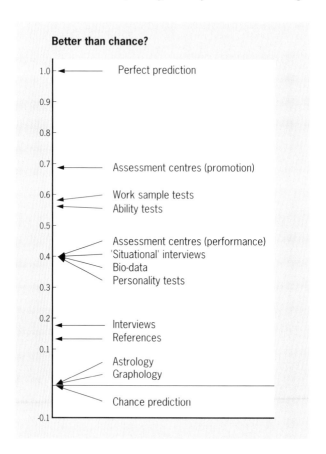

Figure 4.1 *Selection methods and job performance*

Source: *Torrington et al.* (1995)

We cover interviews and testing in some detail in this theme, but we also look at other aspects of the selection process, including creating a shortlist of candidates and taking up final references.

You will:

◆ **Consider how to compile a shortlist that is objective and takes account of equality and diversity issues**

- ◆ **Evaluate the case for using testing to improve the reliability and validity of the selection decision**
- ◆ **Identify the key characteristics of an effective interview**
- ◆ **Review the key skills of a good interviewer**
- ◆ **Consider why it is important to take up references.**

Creating a shortlist

Your objective in creating a shortlist is to identify those applicants who most closely fit the person specification. The most common problem with shortlisting is inconsistency – relating to both the people you involve and the process you use.

The people

Avoid inconsistency by ensuring those involved in shortlisting are involved every step of the way – through to final selection of the most suitable person. Ideally, they will be the same people involved in developing the job description and person specification. This involvement builds ownership and consistency into the decision-making process.

The process

The process itself can also fall down if you have not clearly defined the selection criteria. Everyone must know what to look for when examining an application. Therefore, they may need training on how to shortlist and they will certainly find it useful to have shortlisting documentation. This documentation contains the criteria against which people will be judged, with essential factors first. This allows everyone to judge each applicant against the same relevant, weighted criteria.

Applying consistent criteria

Using shortlisting documentation aids decision making and is good equal opportunities practice. Decide and agree beforehand what you are looking for. The following are some examples.

What matters most?

The most important features you have to assess are how closely the information provided matches the essential criteria for the job. You are paying particular attention to the person's experience and qualifications. When looking at experience, look for what has been achieved rather than a straight description of the role.

It's important to bear in mind that relevant experience may come from outside work, particularly in the case of an applicant who has been away from the workplace for some time.

Outside interests are also important in assessing applicants. For example, many people display skills of leadership, teamworking and self-starting abilities through hobbies and interests. Examples include being a school governor, captaining a sports team or undertaking a course of study through evening classes.

Look at the language people use. Is it precise, such as 'managed', 'led' and 'achieved', or is it vague, such as 'involved in', 'was part of' or 'liaised with'? Precise language usually indicates a high level of involvement.

You may have asked applicants to assess their own suitability for the post, and if this is the case, this part will need to be reviewed carefully. Look at this in terms of how the applicants explain how they are suited to the job.

There are certain factors that should be justified – if not on the application, then most certainly at the selection stage. Examples include long periods of unemployment, frequent job changes over a short space of time, a drop in salary when moving from one job to the next or a number of sideways moves. These are not always negative, but you will need to question why this is the case.

Be careful that discrimination and bad practice don't creep in at this stage. No applicant should be rejected on the grounds of gender, marital or family status, ethnicity or nationality, age, disability or overseas qualification. You could also discriminate unfairly against people if you introduce new or different criteria after the applications have been received. Similarly, bad practice can arise if selectors are swayed by factors such as use of language, handwriting and, above all, gut instinct.

How not to shortlist
In a transport company, 80 per cent of decisions – reject or consider further – can be predicted from nine facts: maths grade (at A level), degree in maths or computer science, experience in a transport organisation, belonging to societies related to transport, work experience in computer programming, having been on an 'Insight into Management' course. People who wrote a lot were considered further, as were people who wrote neatly, and people who use 'certain (unspecified) keywords'. People from certain parts of Britain (also unspecified) were more likely to be rejected.

Source: *Cook* (1993)

Building a shortlist

The following steps will help you ensure the shortlisting process is fair and consistent:

- People involved in sifting and sorting meet to agree the shortlisting criteria and are provided with shortlisting documentation.
- Each person shortlists on essential factors, with desirable factors being used if too many applicants meet the essential ones.
- Each shortlister decides whether a person should be called in or not and writes down their reasons.
- The group meets together to pull together the final list of candidates and the decisions are recorded as to why a person is being shortlisted.
- The group also records reasons for rejection. This is important because, should the decision ever be the subject of legal action, you'll need to be able to justify your choice.

Recently ... the emphasis has changed from screening. It is now a question of deciding who should be included rather than who should be eliminated. This is not a semantic quibble, but an important change in looking for the positive aspects rather than the negative.

Source: *Torrington and Hall* (1998)

Telephone shortlisting

From its *Recruitment, retention and turnover survey 2004* the CIPD found that 26% of organisations, particularly those in the service sector, use telephone interviews to shortlist candidates quickly based on essential criteria such as employment objective, education and required skills, or as a test of telephone skills. The survey found that telephone interviewing is not being used as a replacement for face-to-face interviews and is largely used for shortlisting either in place of or alongside a traditional application form.

What to do next

Once the final shortlist has been agreed, you must contact successful applicants with all the relevant information they need. This includes date, time, duration and place of the interview plus the details of any assessment or testing that will take place and why this is relevant. Candidates may also need a location map plus instructions about what to do on arrival. It is also courteous to ask if they have any special needs such as dietary requirements or building access.

It is also good practice to contact unsuccessful candidates and provide them with the opportunity to request feedback if required.

A poor response

If you have too few applicants, it is important to analyse what went wrong.

♦ Is the job description a true reflection of the job?

♦ Does the person specification clearly match the job description or are your expectations too high?

♦ Is the salary too low for the role, the skill level required and/or market conditions?

♦ Did you market the role widely or were you too restrictive?

♦ Did the advertising copy give a positive yet realistic impression of the organisation and the role?

♦ Were the essential criteria used for shortlisting the correct ones?

♦ Was processing of applications timely and efficient?

Activity 13
Shortlisting

Objective

This activity will help you to review your department's shortlisting procedures.

Case study

The following shows how not to shortlist.

Let me have a go

Two managers sat down together to look at a pile of application forms for a job in marketing. One was the HR manager who had been involved in analysing the job, developing the specifications and advertising. The other was the marketing manager who would be responsible for the new recruit.

As they sat down, in walked the marketing director. 'Let me have a look at what we've got. After all I'm the one in charge of the department. I should have some say.' The two managers looked at one another, but made no comment.

The HR manager began to explain the criteria for the post and how to score the candidates. 'I don't need that,' said the marketing director. 'I've been here long enough to tell good from bad. I know what I'm looking for. You get an instinct for it.'

More significant glances between the managers, and silence fell on the room.

An hour later the three came together to compare notes.

'Well,' said the director, 'I'll tell you what I've done. I've rejected those two because the forms are impossible to read as they're so untidy. Full of spelling mistakes. That one's too old. He was in school in the 1960s! Probably remembers England winning the World Cup! This girl sounds well qualified but I bet she leaves to have kids, or worse still, will expect us to pay her for having kids. Those two have foreign qualifications. Don't know how they'd stand up here. So it's down to these four.'

'Why have you chosen them?' the HR manager dared to ask.

'Well, he has a lot of experience and enjoys rugby. She's fairly inexperienced but is doing an MBA. I'd love to do an MBA. He's also lacking somewhat in experience, but went to the same university as me. And these two can make up the numbers.'

'Have you documented all your reasons for your choices?' asked the HR manager.

'Don't need to, old boy. It's all in my head. It's easy this shortlisting lark, isn't it?'

Task

1   Using the case study as an example of how not to shortlist, make a list of good practice in shortlisting.

Good practice steps in shortlisting:

2 How do your ideas differ from those used in your organisation?
Highlight areas where your organisation falls down and make
recommendations.

My recommendations are:

Feedback

Your good practice steps may include the following points:

◆ Involve the same people throughout the process – from analysis to reaching the final decision

◆ Make sure everyone is trained and briefed

◆ Agree essential criteria at an early stage – never introduce additional criteria once applications have been received

◆ Apply essential criteria first before moving on to desirable factors

◆ Use shortlisting documentation

◆ Check that applicants are not assessed against irrelevancies such as age, marital status, handwriting or hobbies

◆ Ensure those making the shortlist can justify their decisions – for and against candidates.

Don't be swayed in your decision by a senior person on the shortlisting panel.

The testing option

Testing is used by some organisations to distinguish between candidates. This is because interviews alone are poor at predicting job performance.

There are so many tests available, claiming to assess so many factors, that the choices you have can seem overwhelming. If the right tests are chosen and properly administered, they can help you enormously in appointing the most suitable candidate. On the other hand, inappropriate testing can have the opposite effect and, in the worst cases, lead to claims of discrimination resulting in the intervention of an industrial tribunal.

If you are considering using a test the following points are important:

◆ It must test what it claims to test – it must be valid

◆ It must give consistent results – it must be reliable

◆ It must be easy to administer and score

◆ Its purpose must be clear to all who undertake it

◆ It must be cost-effective

◆ It must not be discriminatory.

You should never introduce tests without the support of expert help, such as a human resource specialist.

Testing options

Your choices are many and varied.

Ability tests. You can use ability tests to measure a person's current skills and ability to meet the demands of the job. These tests are often designed in-house and can be paper based and completed by post before the interview. They can be a good way of asking a candidate to demonstrate some of the skills required.

Aptitude tests. These measure potential rather than current or past performance. They can test factors such as verbal reasoning or mental ability, or they can cover areas specific to a role. You might find aptitude tests useful if you are appointing on competencies or if the duties of the job are likely to change.

Trainability tests. You can use these to measure a person's potential to be trained. It usually involves asking the candidate to undertake an activity they have never done before, having received some instruction first.

Personality tests. These are among the most controversial tests as there is a wide range of opinion as to what personality is, let alone its impact at work. There are also more tests available in this category than any others. One of the dangers is that candidates may not be honest in their answers. If someone regularly takes these tests, they may even know what answers to provide to gain the highest marks.

Work sample tests. In this case candidates undertake some of the tasks or are faced with some of the problems they may meet on the job. Common examples of these are sales presentations for sales staff, or for office workers, the in-tray exercise where candidates are required to read and action a series of documents they might come across at work.

One test used in isolation can lead to a poor choice of candidate for the job.

Bringing different methods together

A popular way to assess candidates is to hold an assessment centre. It means delivering a series of different tests to a group of people being assessed for the same or similar jobs over one or two days. An assessment centre might include group work, discussions, role-plays, presentations and interviews. They can be designed to assess both suitability and potential, and are widely used for recruitment and promotion to management posts.

On the positive side, they provide all candidates with an opportunity to demonstrate their strengths in a range of situations to a range of people. From your point of view, this is an opportunity to see skills demonstrated rather than being told about them. On the negative side, they are costly to set up, train for and administer.

> In spite of the disadvantages, performance in assessment centres does generally correlate more highly with eventual job performance than does performance in other selection methods.

Source: *Torrington et al.* (1995)

Just how predictable?

Selection methods in call centres

Russell Drakeley, managing director of consultancy Craig, Greg and Russell (CGR), which has been involved with call centres since they first appeared in the UK, says an increasing amount of research points to the fact that personality testing during the selection process can pay dividends...

Surprisingly (CGR's own) research shows that initial assumptions made about the kind of person who would make the ideal centre worker – or 'agent' as they are known – were way off track. It has found that far from the bubbly, chatty extrovert being the perfect personality, introverts are actually better suited to the kind of work involved...

Steve Blinkhorn of Psychometric Research & Development, which has formulated a range of psychometric ability tests, including the Able series published by Oxford Psychological Press, argues that personality is of little relevance when selecting staff for call centres...

An alternative method of assessment that has proved its worth in call centres is the use of work samples or simulations. CGR has itself developed a tailored work sample test for Greater Manchester police. This has been used successfully for five years at the force's emergency call centre.

A similar but subtler approach is to use a structured learning exercise, which Blinkhorn has been developing for several years. These differ from standard simulations or work sample tests in their emphasis on the learning process... But the system makes no attempt to assess personality. People who work in call centres need to be able to handle repetitive work, pay attention to detail, learn quickly and not be afraid of technology, he argues. Beyond that any search for the ideal type of call centre personality is pointless...

Drakeley counters this by stressing that personality testing is only part of a bigger battery of techniques used for selection. His company would never rely on one test alone. 'There is now a body of opinion that there are good and bad personality questionnaires,' he says. 'If you've got a good questionnaire and use it properly, it adds to the kind of information you can obtain from other assessments.'

One thing is clear: there is no shortage of assessment tools being developed specifically for this market, so people will have plenty of choice.

Source: *Whitehead* (1999)

Psychometrics and the law
Using psychometric testing in recruitment processes could land employers in court... Giles Proctor, senior law lecturer at Manchester Metropolitan University's law school, describes the popular tests as 'potentially problematic' under Article 8 of the Human Rights Act (HRA), which deals with respect for privacy, family life and correspondence... Patricia Leighton, head of the law school, said a number of human rights were likely to have a major effect on the recruitment process.

'Any job applicant has profoundly important rights to privacy, freedom of expression, religion and freedom of correspondence,' Leighton said. 'This will inhibit the inquiries you can make on application forms.'

The EU Burden of Proof Directive ... covers both the recruitment process and the workplace. It will, for the first time, put the onus on employers to prove that discrimination did not take place... Article 13 of the EU Amsterdam Treaty, which calls for equal treatment regardless of religion, belief, age or sexual orientation, is also expected to have an impact on job advertisements and on employment terms and conditions...

As Leighton says, 'The restrictions the law is putting on the recruitment process as we have known it leaves three things that recruiters should seek: qualifications, experience and skills.'

Source: *Rana* (2000)

Activity 14
Selection tests

Objective

Use this activity to:

◆ review a selection test your organisation uses and check it is fit for its purpose, or

◆ recommend the introduction of a selection test for a particular role.

Task

1 Choose one selection test that is currently used for recruitment in your department or organisation. Use the checklist below to assess its value.

2 If you do not use selection tests, choose one job where a test may be helpful. Find information on a number of tests and use the checklist to assess which one would be of most value.

Selection tests – checklist

1	It is appropriate for the job in question	☐
2	It has standardised measures	☐
3	It begins with easy tasks/activities and moves on to more difficult ones	☐
4	It is valid in that it measures what it is supposed to measure	☐
5	It has clear instructions to follow	☐
6	It is supported by full documentation	☐
7	It has a history in that it has been used for similar jobs before	☐
8	It is reliable in that it always measures the same thing	☐
9	It is fair and non-discriminatory	☐
10	It is cost-effective	☐

Note your conclusions here:

Feedback

If the test fails on any of the points in the checklist, you need to seriously consider whether the test should be used at all. There may be something more appropriate on the market and new tests are being developed all the time.

Seek out specialist advice on the subject and talk to other managers in the business or from same-sector organisations to find out what they use. If you contact any providers yourself, you can use the checklist as a basis for finding out more information.

Interviews

While many organisations are using testing as part of their selection procedures, the interview is still at the heart of most processes.

Types of interview

Selection interviewing in Europe
It is interesting to contrast different approaches to selection in different countries. Bulois and Shackleton (1996) note that interviews are the cornerstone of selection activity in both Britain and France, but that they are consciously used in different ways.

In Britain they argue that interviews are increasingly structured and criterion-referenced, whereas in France the approach tends to be deliberately unstructured and informal. They note that in France the premise is that 'the more at ease the candidates are, the higher the quality of their answer', whereas in Britain they characterise the premise as 'the more information you get about an individual, the better you know him/her and the more valid and reliable your judgement is'.

Tixier (1996) in a survey covering the EU (but excluding France), Switzerland, Sweden and Austria, found that structured interviews were favoured in the UK, Scandinavia, Germany and Austria. This contrasted with Italy, Portugal, Luxembourg and Switzerland where unstructured styles were preferred.

Source: *Torrington and Hall* (1998)

Structured interviews

A structured interview typically has three characteristics:

◆ The questions are developed from the job analysis and are based on the job description, person specification or competence framework

◆ Each candidate is asked the standard though not necessarily identical questions

◆ A systematic scoring system is used.

Structured interviews aim to replicate the standardised and scientific nature of tests, but there are issues. Some candidates are extremely good at articulating their achievements and plans but might not put these into practice. The converse is also true.

One-to-one and panel interviews

One-to-one interviews are common and you may find they're appropriate for unskilled or semi-skilled posts where the job is unlikely to change or develop. The difficulty is that one person will be making all the decisions. While you may think it's an economic option, this is not the case if the wrong person is appointed and leaves you within the first few months.

What you'll find is that in the majority of cases, and particularly for management, technical and new roles, a panel interview is best. It not only broadens the decision-making process, but it is seen to be fair.

However, panel interviewing brings its own challenges, for example, if panellists are not clear about their own role and how to question candidates. In addition, one interviewer may try to dominate the interview and there is a danger that if you can't all reach consensus, a 'compromise candidate' may be appointed.

Preparing for an interview

Everyone involved needs to be clear about what it is you're trying to achieve. This is more than just grilling each candidate to find out who best matches the specification. It's also about providing candidates with sufficient information to let them decide if they want to work for you. You also want to leave people with a positive impression of your organisation – whether or not they are appointed. Table 4.1 shows how highly candidates regard good interview preparation.

> **Leave people with a positive impression of your organisation.**

Interviewer not prepared or focused	39%
Lack of feedback on status	38%
Inconsistent, or no concrete description of job description	37%
Being kept waiting an unreasonable amount of time	37%
Next step unclear	23%
Process too long and complicated	17%

Table 4.1 *Job candidates see these problems in the interview process*

Source: *Integrity Search Inc.* (1998)

You have to make sure that interviewers are clear about how the selection criteria will be weighted. In other words, which criteria are essential and which are desirable.

You need to assign responsibility in terms of who asks what. This means that basic questions should be prepared for each factor/criterion – both main questions and likely follow-ups. This does not mean that additional questions cannot be used to probe for further detail, but these basic questions will establish the standard for questioning each candidate you see.

You will also need to check that everyone has been trained in interviewing skills and techniques.

Interviewers must also be encouraged to keep to time. It gives a poor impression to run over the allotted time, and there must be space between each candidate for interviewers to record their comments.

In terms of practicalities, make sure that your interview room is quiet, private, well lit and accessible. Make sure the room is set out to put people at ease. Avoid barriers such as desks, if at all possible, and make sure you won't be interrupted. Also check arrangements have been made to greet each candidate and offer refreshments.

Conducting the interview

Welcome the candidate

Greet each candidate by name. Introduce yourselves and thank them for coming. Ask them about their journey to put them at ease. Explain what kind of interview it is going to be, how long you expect it to take and its format. Ask if they have any questions before you start. Setting the scene in this way and involving them at an early stage helps to remove early tensions.

Collect the detail you need

The same interviewer should put the same basic questions to all candidates. This ensures fairness in the interview process, but should not rule out asking supplementary questions to probe for information. Make sure you ask each candidate to supply specific examples/evidence of their experience and abilities to show how they are suited to the role.

Record relevant information

Make a note of key information and explain to the candidates what you are doing and why. Do not rely on memory. You don't need to make copious notes, but do record all essential information – in particular, evidence which highlights the ways in which they meet the essential criteria. The format shown in Table 4.2 is a possible method for structuring notes.

Records are useful for several reasons:

- To jog your memory when you compare candidates before reaching your final decision

- To help interviewers recall information when giving feedback to unsuccessful candidates

- To have a record of proceedings for protection if a candidate accuses you of discrimination.

Candidate		
Criteria and weighting	Grade/ assessment	Evidence/ comments

Table 4.2 *Recording information*

Answer candidates' questions

Candidates often leave the interview feeling they have been pumped for information and received nothing in return. In other words, they have had no opportunity to find out what they need to know about the job and the organisation. Take time to answer questions fully and beware of giving an unrealistic assessment of the job and the business. If you do this and the reality is very different, the new appointee may not stay with you long.

Close the interview

Cover these issues as the interview is brought to a close:

- 'Do you have any further questions about the job or our work?'

- 'If we offered you the job, would you accept it?'

- 'I'll explain to you now what happens next in terms of reaching a decision.'

Reaching a decision

After all the candidates have been interviewed, you will make a joint decision. Meet as a group and provide everyone with the opportunity to discuss their opinions. This can be time-consuming but if everyone is briefed as to what you are looking for, consensus should not take too long. When a decision has been made, record your reasons for selection and non-selection.

Activity 15
Improving interviews

Objective

Use this activity to assess a recorded interview and identify areas for improvement.

Case study

Read the following dialogue from an interview.

> **The fifth interview**
>
> 'Ah come in Mr, em, Mathews. Oh sorry it's Mr James. Sorry we're all a bit shell-shocked at present. You're the fifth one we've seen today you know. Bit of a mammoth task this. Sorry to have kept you waiting so long. Got a bit behind. Sorry. Now where's your application?' (Interviewer shuffles papers, while one of the other four people on the panel stifles a yawn.) 'Got them. Right. Raj, would you like to start the questions this time?'
>
> 'Right Mr James, my name is Raj Patel. I'll be your line manager, should you be selected for this post. I'd like to begin by asking...' (Raj asks a series of open and probing questions that produce very pertinent answers from the candidate. However, they are interrupted twice by mobile phones going off.)
>
> 'Thank you, Mr James. I'll pass the questioning to Mrs Brown, who is the operations director.'
>
> 'Thanks Raj. I hope you don't mind me asking, but I see you have a young family. How would they feel about relocating to Swindon? Any family commitments in Carlisle?' (Mr James answers but Mrs Brown doesn't really listen to the answer. She sits back in her chair and folds her arms.)

(The interview continues for some time – with the candidate being asked questions in a seemingly random fashion.)

'Thank you Mr James. Do you have any questions of your own?'

'No, I don't.'

'Well what happens now is we compare each of you against the criteria for the job and make our final decision. You will hear within five days. One final point. If we were to offer you this job, subject to references, would you take it?'

'To be perfectly honest, I wouldn't work here if it was the last place on earth. As far as I see it, you are the weakest link. Goodbye.'

Task

1 What are the good points about this interview?

2 What lessons can be learned from the things that went wrong during the interview?

The good points are:	The lessons that can be learned are:

Feedback

You may agree that, unfortunately, there were far more bad points than good ones. See how your ideas compare:

Good points

◆ There clearly were criteria for the job

◆ It was a panel interview, which is better than one-to-one as decisions are more likely to be objective

◆ Raj introduced himself, as did Mrs Brown

◆ Raj asked some good open and probing questions

◆ The next steps were explained.

Possible lessons to be learned

◆ Don't overwhelm the candidate – five people is a very large panel

◆ Introduce people properly – only two of the panel introduced themselves

◆ Take time to build rapport – this panel went straight into questioning

◆ Be organised – calling somebody by the wrong name and hunting for their application is unacceptable

◆ Treat every interviewee as if he or she is the first – this sounds as if Mr James is going through some sort of car auction

◆ Know in advance who will ask what – these questions were delivered in a random order

◆ Don't hold too many interviews in a day – five is probably too many

◆ Be aware of how you come across – Mrs Brown's folded arms and her leaning back could come across as a sign of boredom or disinterest

◆ Plan the time carefully – poor Mr James was called in late

◆ Stay professional – however tempting it may be to yawn or answer your mobile phone

◆ Don't ask discriminatory questions – Mr James' family commitments should be of no interest to the panel.

Effective interview questioning

Effective questioning is the method by which you obtain information from each candidate to enable you to reach a decision. You need to plan questions in advance – both in terms of what to ask and what not to ask. Poor questioning may mean the wrong person is appointed and can also lead to discrimination.

Types of question

Open questions are often most useful in an interview situation. These encourage a candidate to talk as they cannot be answered 'yes' or 'no'. Open questions normally start with 'what', 'when', 'where', 'how', 'who' or 'why'. However, do take care when using 'why' as it can provoke a defensive reply.

In addition to straightforward open questions, use the following types of question to obtain more detail.

Probing questions. These allow candidates to develop their initial answers. You use them to follow up the answer to one question with another open question. This can be a supplementary question or the first question put in a different way. They are particularly useful to find out what lies behind an answer. For example: *'Why did you feel that hadn't gone as well as expected?'*

Reflective questions. Here you rephrase an answer as another question and send it back to the interviewee. You can use it to check understanding or to encourage expansion of a previous answer. For example: *'When you say you were successful, what was your benchmark?'*

Hypothetical questions. These are the 'what if' questions. They're designed to assess a candidate's ability to handle particular situations related to the job. For example: *'If that situation arose again, what would you do differently?'*

Encouraging questions. You can use these to express interest in a particular area of a candidate's experience to draw out further information. They perform a similar function to probing questions but are particularly useful with timid candidates. For example: *'I'm fascinated by your work with the youth club. How would you say the skills you use there may be of value in this new role?'*

Closed questions. These tend to lead to a short 'yes', 'no' or 'don't know' answer. We tend to use closed questions as part of normal conversation. You can use them in an interview to check understanding, summarise, bring the conversation back to the point if it has gone off track and to close the interview.

What do you hope to find out?

Here are some examples of topics you may want to cover in an interview. However, bear in mind these are very general and will probably not all be appropriate for the role for which you're recruiting. Your questions should be designed to establish whether or not the candidate can display specific evidence of the key competencies necessary to perform the job.

General areas of questioning:

♦ major achievements in previous role

♦ goal setting and methods of achieving goals

♦ demonstrating ability to deal with challenges and problems

♦ decision making under pressure

♦ time management and organisational abilities

♦ setting priorities and dealing with conflicting priorities

♦ use of communication skills to get a point across or persuade others to change

♦ motivation of colleagues and subordinates

♦ dealing with poor performance

♦ ability to be flexible/adaptable

♦ demonstrating creativity or flair

♦ demonstrating influencing skills

♦ contribution to teamwork

♦ describing a problem and how this was overcome.

When questioning, listen out for examples of behaviours that confirm what the candidate is telling you.

Questions to avoid and why

There is a range of questions that you must avoid at interview. This is because they represent poor interviewing techniques or because they can result in discrimination.

What to avoid

Leading questions. These are questions that are phrased in such a way that the person is forced to provide the answer you want to hear. For example: *'It seems to me that this is an example of performing over and above the requirements of the role. Wouldn't you agree?'*

Critical questions. Questions that bring the person's ability, skill or judgement into question should be avoided. They can undermine the confidence of even the most promising candidate. You do have to probe; you do not have to be personal. For example: *'This would*

indicate that you lack some of the skills required of a good team player, wouldn't it?'

Multiple questions. This arises when several questions are put together, leading to confusion and a poor response. For example: *'Would you say you have strong problem-solving skills? Does the example you have outlined highlight this and how can what you have learned from that experience be applied to future situations?'*

Discriminatory questions. These questions have overtones of discrimination, bias or stereotyping. These are not only unfair, but can lead to very public consequences should a candidate decide to take things further. Questions that have the potential of being discriminatory are usually about issues such as:

◆ marital status

◆ family/carer responsibility

◆ gender

◆ race

◆ disability and ability to undertake the role

◆ age.

Potentially discriminatory questions
While there are many questions that can lead to accusations of discrimination, the following are common examples.

'There are very few women working here. Do you think you could cope?'

'Does your condition mean you need to take time off to visit a doctor?'

'I see you're recently married. Do you intend to have children in the near future?'

'You live rather a long way away and don't drive. With the shift patterns here, will you be all right going to and from work in the dark?'

'We don't have anyone else here from an ethnic minority. Will you be able to cope with the jokes and banter?'

'You're older than most of our staff. How do you think you'll fit in?'

'What arrangements have you made for childcare while you're at work?'

Almost a quarter of workers and those who have left the labour market recently agree (either strongly or slightly) with the statement 'In my industry employers aren't interested in employing or promoting people over the age of 40.' Among younger respondents aged 16–24 perceptions of age discrimination in the workplace are more widespread with 37% in agreement that this is the case.

Source: *Compton-Edwards* (2001)

Sample interview questions

'What would you say was your major achievement in your previous job?'

'What would be an example of an important goal you set yourself in the past and how did you go about achieving it?'

'What do you do when faced with a problem that tests your ability to cope? Give an example.'

'How do you go about reaching decisions in pressurised situations?'

'What did you do in your last role to ensure you were effective with your planning and organising?'

'How do you deal with conflicting priorities? Use examples to illustrate your point.'

'How would you use your communication skills to get your point across when others are in disagreement with you?'

'How do you go about motivating colleagues and subordinates when you are all under pressure?'

Interviewing skills

Interviewing is more than asking pertinent questions. It is also about listening carefully to what you are told and interpreting the information you receive, through both oral and non-verbal communication. This section examines the interviewing techniques of listening, body language and note taking.

Listening skills

Listening is harder than we think. This is partly because the brain can process information faster than someone can talk. Research shows that we remember only 30 per cent of what we hear. Here are some common traits that people display when listening:

- hearing only what we expect to hear
- making assumptions about what the other person means
- becoming distracted
- interrupting to make a point
- finishing someone's sentence for them.

The following points may help:

- Sit up straight and maintain eye contact with the interviewee, without staring. Nod and smile appropriately as they answer your questions.
- Avoid being distracted by things around you – a ringing phone, a ticking clock or what's going on outside the window.
- Make notes to help you concentrate on relating the answer you are hearing to the question you posed.
- Mentally pick out the key issues they are emphasising.
- Ask questions to clarify any unclear responses and summarise what has been said to check you understand.
- Allow the other person time to speak. Don't hurry them or finish their sentences for them.
- Remember silences are part of the process – they allow the candidate time to formulate their answer.
- Avoid formulating your next question until the present one has been fully answered.
- Listen to the tone of voice. A high pitch may indicate an emotional response, while a dull tone may indicate lack of interest.
- Listen for certain words or phrases that may indicate lack of conviction, such as 'I should have...', 'I might have...' or 'I tried but...'

Active listening is as much about questioning as it is about hearing what is being said. Through skilful questioning you send signals to the other person that you are interested in what they are saying and this in turn leads them to relax and talk more freely.

Body language

Less than 10 per cent of a first impression is created by what we say. As a good interviewer, you need to pay attention to body language as it can reflect the candidate's real feelings about something. It is equally important to pay attention to your own body language – or you may betray your own thoughts about a candidate before giving them a fair chance.

The importance of body language

If the language of the rest of the body appears to contradict what the mouth is saying, we should not believe the mouth.

Language is the most sophisticated product of the human intellect, and we spend much effort in refining and controlling our use of it. The rest of the body is a complex and comparatively primitive entity, over which we can only exercise partial control. If it indicates something different from our words, it is virtually certain to be nearer the truth.

The interviewer must learn to look closely for signs of unexpected tension or other spontaneous actions when interviewing. We will rarely see the candidate actually squirm when we probe a particular point, but we may well observe tension or anxiety in the hands or eyes, or by a shift of posture.

If the candidate expresses keen interest in some aspect of the job, or agrees with a statement we make, we will watch to see if his posture and expression tell the same story.

Source: *Peel* (1998)

> **38% of all communication is tone of voice, 55% is body language and only 7% is the words we use.**
>
> **Mehrabian and Ferris (1967)**

Be aware of the following aspects of body language:

◆ Body orientation – facing you or turning the body towards you is generally a positive sign of interest and involvement. Sudden changes in orientation suggest a sudden change in reaction.

◆ Posture – an upright posture is preferable to someone slumped in the chair as it suggests the person is alert and interested.

◆ Eye contact – looking at you without staring is positive. So is making eye contact with each member of the interview panel. You need to be aware, however, that in some cultures, avoiding eye contact is actually a sign of respect.

◆ Head and facial movements – these should match what the person is saying. For example, answering a question positively, yet shaking the head from side to side gives out contradictory signals.

While you're interpreting non-verbal communication signals from candidates, it's equally important to be aware of the messages you transmit – see Table 4.3.

Positive signals	Negative signals
Sitting in an open position with legs and arms uncrossed	Folding your arms or sitting in a hunched position
Turning your body towards the person	Fiddling – with paper, rings or pens or 'doodling' when someone is talking
Being aware of their comfort zone in terms of how close you sit	Yawning, looking bored or letting your eyes wander
Making positive eye contact without staring	Shuffling and constantly changing body position
Nodding, smiling and making listening noises to help build rapport and show encouragement	Smiling inappropriately when someone is making a serious point

Table 4.3 *Be aware of your own non-verbal communication*

Note taking

Note taking is essential. Notes may be taken by a specially appointed scribe so that you can focus on the interview itself, but often it will be up to you to make your own notes. You'll have to record key points, which will be used to complete the selection documentation and help you in reaching a decision.

Make notes at the side of each question. This helps to prevent you from asking a question further down the list which has already been answered. It can also prompt you to probe more deeply if the first answer is unsatisfactory.

◆ Use only key words or abbreviated notes while the interviewee is speaking. It can be distracting if all the interviewee sees is the top of your head.

◆ Use underlining or asterisks to highlight important areas of your notes. Avoid using ticks and crosses as the candidate may feel they are being marked and lose confidence.

◆ Make sure your notes cover facts and not opinion.

Remaining unbiased

No interviewer is completely free from bias. It's quite natural that you feel more empathy with some people than others. The skill is in recognising that this can happen and trying to give the same level of objectivity to all candidates.

Common sources of bias include the following:

Physical attractiveness. There is evidence to show that people who are physically attractive are viewed more favourably than those who are not, irrespective of their gender.

Personal liking. If a person has similar attitudes, beliefs and background to you, you are more likely to regard them in a

Favourable light. This can include having the same hobbies or going to similar schools and colleges – all of which bears no relationship to their ability to do the job.

Halo and horns effect. It is very easy to judge a candidate as all good (halo) or all bad (horns), when in fact everyone has both good and bad features. It happens when a candidate has one outstanding characteristic and the interviewer tries to minimise all the other, opposite characteristics.

Primacy bias. It's easy to be influenced by information obtained early in the interview, whether positive or negative. The interviewer establishes their opinion in the first three minutes and spends the rest of the session trying to justify their belief.

Contrast effect. This happens when a candidate is judged by the standard of the preceding couple of interviewees. For example, if an average candidate follows two weak ones, the average candidate is judged as strong when in fact they are not.

Activity 16
Identifying interviewing skills

Objective

Use this activity to identify the strengths and weaknesses in your interviewing skills.

Task

Use the following checklist to assess your interviewing skills.

Tick either **H** (high level of skill), **M** (moderate level of skill) or **L** (low level of skill or non-existent).

Skill	H	M	L
Greeting candidates in a friendly way	☐	☐	☐
Building rapport	☐	☐	☐
Relating a question to the relevant criteria	☐	☐	☐
Asking open questions	☐	☐	☐
Asking probing questions to obtain information	☐	☐	☐
Using closed questions when appropriate	☐	☐	☐
Explaining things to people	☐	☐	☐
Listening actively to what is being said	☐	☐	☐
Feeling comfortable with silences and pauses	☐	☐	☐

Skill	H	M	L
Avoiding becoming distracted	☐	☐	☐
Taking clear and concise notes	☐	☐	☐
Relating notes to the criteria	☐	☐	☐
Making positive eye contact	☐	☐	☐
Using positive body language	☐	☐	☐
Interpreting the body language of the candidate	☐	☐	☐
Being aware of possible areas for discrimination	☐	☐	☐
Remaining impartial	☐	☐	☐
Keeping people focused on the process	☐	☐	☐
Checking understanding	☐	☐	☐
Managing time to keep the interviews on track	☐	☐	☐

Feedback

Review your checklist and look at those areas where you have ticked 'L'. These are your priorities for development. Review those areas where you have ticked 'M'. Talk to others to see if they would agree with your evaluation. If they do, these might also be areas you wish to develop. This can be through training, coaching or gaining more experience by sitting in on interviews as an observer.

Activity 17
Taking part in interviews

Objective

Use this activity to:

◆ observe an interview or

◆ plan to take part in an interview.

Task

If you are new to interviewing:

Sit in on an interview and use the checklist below to assess what happens. Make notes to summarise the main issues.

If you have some experience of interviews:

Plan and take part in an interview. Use the checklist to evaluate your own and others' performance. Make notes to summarise the main issues.

Planning and preparation	Yes	No
The interviewer(s) had prepared well	☐	☐
They knew who was doing what	☐	☐
The room was set out properly	☐	☐
Timings were about right	☐	☐

Starting well	Yes	No
Each candidate was welcomed	☐	☐
The interviewer(s) introduced themselves	☐	☐
They built rapport with each candidate	☐	☐
The interview format was explained	☐	☐

Interview skills	Yes	No
The interviewer(s) had questions written down	☐	☐
Each person knew who would ask what	☐	☐
Interviewer(s) used open questions	☐	☐
They probed candidates on points of interest	☐	☐
Candidates were asked to provide evidence	☐	☐
Candidates had sufficient time to answer	☐	☐
Interviewer(s) were clearly listening actively	☐	☐
Interviewer(s) seemed skilled at making notes	☐	☐
Candidates' questions were fully answered	☐	☐
Body language was open	☐	☐
Good eye-contact was maintained	☐	☐
The decision process was fully explained	☐	☐
Overall, the interview flowed well	☐	☐

After the interviews	Yes	No
Sufficient time was set aside to discuss candidates	☐	☐
The interviewer(s) had enough information to reach a decision	☐	☐
They clearly related the information to the criteria	☐	☐
Reasoned debate took place	☐	☐
The most suitable candidate was appointed	☐	☐

Notes summarising main issues:

Feedback

If you sat in on an interview, it should have given you the chance to learn from the successes and failures of others. Look at the places where you ticked the no column. Take care that you don't make the same mistakes when you are involved in interviewing.

If you took part in an interview and have ticks in the no column, again you must learn from what went wrong. If there are quite a few ticks, talk it through with your manager. It may be that you need to undertake some training. Selection interviewing is too important to risk making mistakes.

Taking up references

Some organisations take up references for all candidates who are shortlisted but it's more common to only take up references for the candidate who is selected. The job offer is then provisional – based on receipt of satisfactory references.

Reading this section will help you to determine the importance of taking up references.

Why take up references?

While you may be under pressure to fill a vacancy, taking up references is still worth the time and trouble it takes. You have probably invested a great deal of resources to reach this stage, so it is well worth jumping this final hurdle to verify the candidate's credentials.

People leave their previous employer for a number of reasons, the majority of which are totally legitimate. For example, they want a new challenge, they want to increase their salary or they have unfulfilled ambitions that your organisation can provide.

However, their position in their previous organisation may have become untenable because of a poor work record, frequent lateness and absence or, worse still, activity that borders on the criminal such as harassment or theft. Taking up references, therefore, is your final opportunity to find out the truth before employing the individual on a permanent basis.

Creative with the truth?

...there's a fine line between playing up your strengths and misrepresenting your background – and that line, say the experts, is frequently crossed.

'People just flat out lie,' says Val Arnold, senior vice president of executive services at Personnel Decisions Inc., a Minneapolis-based human resources consulting firm.

'We have one client that followed up on a group of resumés and found that well over half had gross exaggerations or outright lies. The candidates were claiming education they didn't have, they were stretching their job responsibilities and, in some cases, if they were involved in a project – suddenly they were running it.'

Source: *Solomon* (1998)

Don't be deterred from taking up references – whatever pressure you are under to fill a post permanently.

Written or oral references?

People usually provide a reference in writing. A former employer is likely to provide factual information about a candidate when requested – dates of employment, salary, duties of the role and absence record.

However, written questions about performance and potential are unlikely to bring much of a response. This is not only because commenting on such matters takes time, but it can also lead to legal pitfalls. While references should be given in confidence, there are legal precedents where contents have been disclosed.

A written reference may invite you to phone if you want any further information. If you are given this opportunity, then take it. It may be that the previous employer has concerns that he or she will not put in writing.

What to look for

The way a reference is written can say quite a lot. It is rare for a previous employer to provide a glowing reference for someone who is appalling – just to get them out of their own organisation. However, a bland and tentative reference can indicate there are potential problem areas.

Some example 'warning signs' are given in Table 4.4.

These statements are not necessarily bad, particularly if these factors are of little importance in the new role. However, they may be things you would like to pursue with the referee by way of a phone call.

Statement	What it might mean
Works well when under pressure	Needs very close supervision
A self-starter who works best alone	Is not a strong team player
Has strong ideas about how work should progress	Does not take the views and opinions of others into account
Requires and requests little management support	Does not work well with authority
Takes the views of all the team into account before deciding on a course of action	Poor at decision making/is indecisive
Works particularly well with close colleagues on the team	Does not work well with other teams

Table 4.4 *Reading into references*

If your suspicions are aroused

Where competition for jobs is fierce, some candidates are not only lenient with the truth, their referees may also be fabricated. From your point of view, there are ways round this.

If you have been given a direct dial number of a senior manager in another organisation and get straight through on the phone, you have a right to be suspicious. People at a senior level rarely answer their own phones. Go through the switchboard instead. If you can't get hold of the main telephone number, the organisation may not exist. If you do get through, the switchboard operator should be able to confirm the referee's name and job title.

If the candidate has come from a large organisation, contact the HR department to check their years of service and job role – although make sure they have already left the organisation before you do this.

You should also probe any claims that the candidate's former organisation has closed down. This may not be the case and can mean the candidate has something to hide. Similarly, if they claim they were made redundant, make sure this is true and they weren't merely fired.

If you suspect bogus qualification claims, check them with the relevant college or school. In today's environment of sophisticated communication, checking overseas qualifications can be just as easy.

◆ Recap

Consider how to compile a shortlist that is objective and takes account of equality and diversity issues

◆ A shortlist is compiled by comparing applicants against the criteria for the job, applying essential criteria first before moving on to desirable factors.

◆ You should record the reasons for shortlisting or rejecting an application so that you can justify your choice.

Evaluate the case for using testing to improve the reliability and validity of the selection decision

◆ Care should be taken to use techniques which are relevant to the job for which you are selecting. All tools used should be validated to ensure their fairness and reliability.

◆ Selection decisions should be based on a range of methods, for example interviews, psychological testing, work sampling exercises and group discussions.

Identify the key characteristics of an effective interview

◆ Interviews should:

– be conducted or supervised by trained individuals

– be structured to follow a previously agreed set of questions mirroring the person specification or job specification

– allow candidates the opportunity to ask questions so that they can decide whether the job suits them.

◆ Interviewers should make notes and record the reasons for selection or non-selection.

Review the key skills of a good interviewer

◆ Interviewers should be skilled in putting candidates at ease and have good communication skills, particularly, listening and questioning.

◆ They need to recognise their own biases so that they can apply the same level of objectivity to all candidates.

Consider why it is important to take up references

◆ References should always be obtained to check factual information on a candidate's employment history, qualifications, experience, timekeeping, performance, etc. They are less useful for collecting subjective opinion as to an applicant's suitability for a job.

▶▶ More @

Roberts, G. (1997) *Recruitment and Selection – A Competency Approach*, CIPD
This book provides details on the whole process of recruitment and selection, including interviewing techniques.

For more information and advice on telephone interviewing, try the website for the *Chartered Institute of Personnel and Development* at **www.cipd.co.uk/subjects/recruitmen/interviews/telintervi.htm? IsSrchRes=1**

Tyson, S., and York, A. (2000) *Essentials of HRM*, Butterworth-Heinemann
Chapter 9 of this text on human resource management explores methods for selecting employees.

Edenborough, R. (2002) *Effective Interviewing: A Handbook of Skills and Techniques*, Kogan Page
This text considers the entire range of interview situations, from selection interviews through to performance interviews, and provides detailed coverage of the methods and techniques currently in practice.

The commercial test provider, **SHL**, publishes its own white papers on selection techniques at www.shl.com/SHL/en-int/ Thought_Leadership/White_Papers/White-Papers.htm

Woodruffe, C. (2000) *Development and Assessment Centres*, CIPD
This is a practical guide to the design and implementation of assessment centres.

5 Making a good start

Induction makes your role, as a line manager, easier as it helps the new employee settle in. Induction helps a new employee to learn about the organisation and its policies. It is the time when they can learn about the job in more detail and you can identify any training and development that may be required. It is also a way of explaining and reinforcing the rules and regulations under which the employee will work and can form the basis for a formal three-month probationary period. As well as providing the practical information, it also sets the right tone for a professional organisation. Induction is no guarantee, but if a person feels welcomed and comfortable with you, then they are more likely to stay.

> ...those most at risk of leaving are new employees. The term induction crisis has been coined to describe the first 12 months of an employee's service in which he or she is at most risk of leaving. The first 12 weeks will be a particularly acute risk period, but normal stability does not really occur until after 12 months of service. Most organisations will find that, even if their labour turnover rates are in low single figures, labour turnover for the 12 month 'induction crisis' will be about 20%. Good recruitment and selection practices must therefore be concerned with stabilising the risk and managing the integration of the new person into the role.

Source: *Roberts* (1997)

As with every aspect of recruitment, your approach to induction needs to be well planned and systematic.

In this theme you will:

♦ condsider why induction is an important element in the recruitment process, for both the organisation and the new recruit

♦ Identify the features of a good induction process.

The stages of a good induction

Induction has three main stages:

1 Making arrangements for the first day.

2 Providing essential information about the organisation.

3 Learning the job and planning how to address any training needs.

It can take anything from a few days to a period of weeks, but the important point is not to bombard the new person with too much information in the first few days. It is important to get a person up to speed quickly, but avoid information overload.

Proper planning is essential and an induction schedule is a useful tool. You can review the schedule with your new employee to see how things are going and find out what else they need to know. You can easily adapt the form shown in Table 5.1 for your own needs.

Activity	Reason	By whom	By when	Duration	Complete
Explain departmental charts	See where own role fits	Self	03/05	60 minutes	✓
Tour of finance department	Understand processes and meet payroll officer	Sammy	03/05	90 minutes	✓

Table 5.1 *Induction planning document with examples*

Starting arrangements

There is some essential information the new recruit needs before they start. This is often provided as an information pack sent to the person's home. Providing this can create enthusiasm and commitment. It also gives the person confidence – they know what to expect on day one.

Starting arrangements – checklist

Prior to starting work, the new employee needs the following details:

◆ starting date and time of arrival

◆ where to report and who will meet them

◆ security procedures they might need to follow

◆ car parking arrangements

◆ documents to bring along

◆ a timetable for day one and who they will meet

◆ an overview of induction

◆ any relevant location maps

◆ any other relevant information, such as salary, pension forms or medical forms

◆ background information on the organisation and the job

◆ any interesting reports, press releases, news or success stories about the organisation

◆ an employee handbook, if you have one.

Induction into the organisation

You need to make sure the new person learns about the organisation as soon as possible. The person then sees where they 'fit' in the organisation and the contribution they will make to its success. It also fulfils your basic legal obligations in areas such as equal opportunities and health and safety.

The first day or so may be taken up with sorting out 'domestic' arrangements such as break times and the location of the canteen and toilets. You'll also need to issue equipment such as protective clothing, phone and computers. It's also important that you introduce the new person to key colleagues, including other team members and managers with whom they'll have contact.

Once the domestics are sorted out, a full induction to the organisation begins. You can do this separately or in between learning the job. In most cases, the latter is preferable. Undertaking some routine work tasks will help to make the person feel productive, although it's important not to put too many work demands on them too early. Start with simple, routine tasks – a few wins in a new job help boost self-esteem.

Induction to the organisation – checklist
The main areas to cover are as follows:

- organisational overview – size, products and services, organisational structures, organisation charts
- organisational philosophy – mission, objectives, vision, values
- building layout and who sits where
- business unit breakdown – who does what
- customers, competitors and customer service
- policies, systems and procedures
- health and safety, fire procedures, security
- career development – appraisal, development planning, career opportunities
- staff benefits such as social activities, pensions, canteen
- communication – team meetings, bulletin boards, newsletters
- standards of conduct, discipline and grievance
- who to approach for help with, for example, with a work problem or salary difficulties.

Induction into the job

While you may not cover every aspect of induction yourself, you are responsible for making sure it happens. Thorough job induction allows you to:

- clarify expected standards of performance
- explain key tasks and responsibilities, in line with the job description
- look at reporting lines

◆ identify any training and development needs

◆ put in place a development plan to monitor and review progress.

Becoming familiar with the job is clearly essential in getting the best out of a person from an early stage.

As well as explaining the job and its standards, you must assess the new person's capability against the requirements of the role. This can be as simple as reviewing the job description and person specification. You can then assess competence through observation and one-to-one discussion. You will need to put together a prioritised training and development plan that aims to plug any gaps in the person's skill, knowledge and ability.

This can be through a mixture of:

◆ on-the-job training

◆ coaching

◆ experiential learning

◆ attending formal training courses

◆ reading

◆ work shadowing.

> Trainees learn only 16% of what they read; 20% of what they see; 30% of what they are told; 50% of what they see and are told and 70% of what they see, are told and respond to; and 90% of what they do.

> Source: *Whitley* (1995)

While you may not be able to monitor progress daily, it's important that the new starter has all the support they need. A 'buddy' system is one method. This means pairing them with a current employee at a similar level who can help them settle in. In addition, the new person will need feedback on progress. Providing this feedback clearly falls within your remit as their manager. It's useful to have a more formal review at the end of the formal probation period. This also helps to set the tone for future performance appraisal interviews.

Providing a contract

You must fulfil your legal obligations by providing a contract of employment within the first few weeks of engagement. In the UK this must be provided by the eighth week. The purpose of the contract is to clarify the employment relationship for both sides.

At a minimum it should include the following elements:

- name of employer and employee
- job title
- date employment began
- salary for the post and when paid, for example, weekly or monthly
- normal contracted hours of work
- entitlement to holiday and holiday pay
- arrangements for sickness reporting
- details of any pension
- notice periods for both parties
- disciplinary and grievance procedures.

Other possible categories of information include:

- confidentiality clauses
- expense entitlement and payment
- company car scheme/car policy
- health and safety obligations
- probation period.

The contract is a legal document and can only be changed for sound business reasons. Therefore it is imperative that the exact details of any contract are correct. You should seek legal advice before putting one together if standard contracts don't already exist.

Activity 18
Improving induction

Objectives

Use this activity to:

- review induction in your department or organisation
- make recommendations for improvement.

Task

1 Use the checklist to evaluate induction in your own department or organisation.

2 In the light of your findings, make recommendations as to how it could be improved.

Evaluating induction

Starting arrangements	Yes	No
Before a new employee starts work, on which of the following is he or she given details?		
◆ Starting date and time of arrival	☐	☐
◆ Where to report and who will meet them	☐	☐
◆ Security procedures they might need to follow	☐	☐
◆ Car parking arrangements	☐	☐
◆ Documents to bring	☐	☐
◆ Who they will meet on day one, plus a timetable for day one	☐	☐
◆ An overview of how they will be inducted	☐	☐
◆ Any relevant location maps	☐	☐
◆ Any other relevant information, e.g. salary, pension forms, medical forms	☐	☐
◆ Background information on the organisation and the job plus interesting reports, press releases, news or success stories.	☐	☐

Induction to the organisation	Yes	No
When being inducted into the organisation does the new employee learn about:		
◆ The organisation's size, products and services, structures?	☐	☐
◆ Organisational philosophy – its mission, objectives, vision, values?	☐	☐
◆ Building layout and who sits where?	☐	☐
◆ Business unit breakdown, in terms of which department does what ?	☐	☐
◆ Customers, competitors and customer service?	☐	☐
◆ Policies, systems and procedures?	☐	☐
◆ Health and safety, fire procedures, security?	☐	☐
◆ Career development through appraisal, development planning, career opportunities?	☐	☐
◆ Staff benefits such as social activities, pensions, canteen?	☐	☐
◆ Communication methods, such as team meetings, bulletin boards, newsletters?	☐	☐
◆ Standards of conduct, discipline and grievance?	☐	☐
◆ Who to approach for help, for example, with a work problem or salary difficulties?	☐	☐

Job induction	Yes	No
When being inducted into the job, is the new starter given sufficient detail on:		
◆ Expected standards of performance?	☐	☐
◆ Key tasks and responsibilities?	☐	☐
◆ The training and development they will receive to make them competent in the job?	☐	☐
◆ Any training plan that has been put in place and how progress will be monitored and reviewed?	☐	☐
◆ Their contract of employment?	☐	☐

Feedback

Clearly, what you recommend will depend on your findings. However, the things that tend to go wrong are fairly common. For example, it may be that insufficient time is allocated to the process. It may be that people are thrown into the job on day one, without any real induction into the organisation. Too often new starters do not have an induction plan. Even if they do, operational issues sometimes take over and induction activities do not take place.

All these sorts of problems present a poor image to the new starter. A poor introduction to a new organisation and new job means that they are less likely to stay with you. If that happens, the expensive recruitment process must start all over again.

Therefore, time and resources put into induction is a real investment into the organisation's future.

◆ Recap

Consider why induction is an important element in the recruitment process, for both the organisation and the new recruit

◆ Employees who feel welcome and understand how they will contribute to the future success of the organisation are more likely to stay – remember the costs associated with recruiting and training the organisation's human resource.

◆ A well-planned induction enables new employees to become fully operational quickly and should be integrated with the recruitment process.

Identify the features of a good induction process

◆ During induction a new recruit should receive essential information about the organisation and its procedures, support for learning and an assessment of training needs.

◆ It is a legal requirement to provide employees with a contract of employment. This clarifies the employment relationship and you should ensure that the details are correct.

 More @

Skeats, J. (1996) *Successful Induction*, **Kogan Page**
This is a practical text with checklists, memory joggers and standard letters for managers who want to give employees a good start in an organisation.

The Chartered Institute of Personnel and Development provides an induction checklist at
www.cipd.co.uk/subjects/recruitmen/induction/induction

References

Amin, R. (2003) *Harnessing Workforce Diversity to Raise the Bottom Line*, www.create-research.co.uk

Armstrong, M. (2000) 'Feel the width', *People Management*, 3rd February, CIPD, 38

Beardwell, I. and Holden, L. (1997) 2nd edition, *Human Resource Management*, Pitman Publishing

Bliss, W. (2000) *Cost of turnover*, www.ers.infomart-usa.com/turnoverarticle.htm

Boyatzis, R. E. (1982) *The competent manager: a model for effective performance*, John Wiley and Sons

Chartered Institute of Personnel and Development (2004) *Recruitment, retention and turnover survey 2004*, CIPD

Clements, P. and Spinks, T. (2000) 3rd edition, *The Equal Opportunities Guide*, Kogan Page

Commission for Racial Equality (2001) 'Post Office condemned for discriminatory recruitment practices', News releases, www.cre.gov.uk

Compton-Edwards, M. (2001) *Age Discrimination at Work*, CIPD, February, 4

Cook, M. (1993) 2nd edition, *Personnel Selection and Productivity*, John Wiley and Sons

Cornell University (1999) 'Core Competencies and Behavioural Indicators', *Toolkit for Hiring Top Performers*, www.ohr.cornell.edu/ohr/hr_tools/hiring_toolkit

Department of Trade and Industry (2002) 'Teleworking in the UK', *Labour Market Trends*, www.dti.gov.uk

Eglin, R. (2001) 'Recruiters Use Web to Catch Graduates', *The Sunday Times*, 25 February

Equal Opportunities Commission (2000a) 'Award of £7,000 compensation for sex discrimination confirmed', News releases, www.eco.org.uk

Equal Opportunities Commission (2000) *Inflexibility costs employer £18,000 and a valued employee*, News releases, www.eco.org.uk

Equal Opportunities Commission (2001) 'New poll shows strong backing for family friendly working', News releases, www.eoc.org.uk

Equal Opportunities Commission (2004) 'Why business needs working parents', www.dti.gov.uk

Evans, M. (2001) *Employing people with disabilities*, CIPD

Finn, F. (2000) 'Screen test', *People Management*, 22 June, 43

Graham, H. T. (1995) 8th edition, *Human Resource Management*, Pitman Publishing

Handy, C. (2001) *The Elephant and the Flea: New Thinking for a New World*, Arrow

Integrity Search Inc. (1998) quoted in *Management Review*, September, 6

Ioannou, R. (2001) 'Managing Diversity', *People Management*, 3 May

Joinson, C. (2001) 'Refocusing Job Descriptions', *Human Resource Magazine*, January, 66

Kandola, R. and Fullerton, J. (1998) 2nd edition, *Diversity in Action*, CIPD

Lee, G., Baker, A. and Beard, D. (1998) 'An away match', *People Management*, 14 May, 54

Leighton, P. and Proctor, G. (2001) *Recruiting within the Law*, CIPD

MacKay, I. (1998) *Listening Skills*, CIPD

Martin, M. and Jackson, T. (2000) *Personnel Practice*, CIPD

Mehrabian, A. and Ferris, R. (1967) 'Inference of attitudes from non-verbal communication in two channels', *The Journal of Counselling Psychology*, 31, 248-52

Pearn, M. and Kandola, R. (1993) 2nd edition, *Job Analysis – a manager's guide*, IPM

Peel, M. (1998) *Readymade Interview Questions*, Kogan Page

Rana, E. (2000) 'Psychometrics tests aren't the right stuff, recruiters told', *People Management*, 8 June, 11

Roberts, G. (1997) *Recruitment and Selection – A Competency Approach*, CIPD

Simmons, S. (1996) *Flexible working – a strategic guide to successful implementation and operation*, Kogan Page

Smalley, L. (1998) *Interviewing and Selecting High Performers*, Kogan Page

Smith, D. (2001) 'Economic Outlook', *The Sunday Times*, 18 March

Solomon, B. (1998) 'Too good to be true', *Management Review*, April, 27

Stredwick, J. and Ellis, S. (1998) *Flexible Working Practices*, CIPD

Taylor, S. (1998) *Employee Resourcing*, CIPD

The Telegraph (2001) 'Biomedical Engineer', 29 March

Toplis, J., Dulewicz, V. and Fletcher, C. (1997) *Psychological Testing*, CIPD

Torrington, D. and Hall, L. (1998) 4th edition, *Human Resource Management*, Prentice Hall

Torrington, D., Hall, L., Haylor, I. and Myers, J. (1995) *Employee Resourcing*, IPD

Training Commission (1998) *Classifying the Components of Management Competences*, Training Commission, Sheffield

Whitehead, M. (1999) 'Churning Questions', *People Management*, 30 September, 46-48

Whitley, J. L. quoted in Smalley, L. R. (1995) *Effective Induction and Training*, Kogan Page

Wood, R., Wood, T. and Payne T. (1998) *Competency-based Recruitment and Selection*, John Wiley and Sons